Women
Activists

Women Activists

Challenging the Abuse of Power

Anne Witte Garland

Foreword by Ralph Nader
Introduction by Frances T. Farenthold

The Feminist Press
at The City University of New York
New York

91 90 89   5 4 3 2

Library of Congress Cataloging-in-Publication Data

Garland, Anne Witte.
    Women activists.

    1. Women social reformers—United States—Biography.
2. Women social reformers—Great Britain—Biography.
3. Women in politics—United States.   4. Women in politics
—Great Britain.   I. Title.
HQ1412.G36 1988   305.4'2'0922 [B]   88–401
ISBN 0–935312–79–X
ISBN 0–935312–80–X (pbk.)

Text design by Paula Martinac

Versions of the chapters on Mary Sinclair and Gale Cincotta originally
appeared in the January 1985 and January 1986 "Women of the Year"
issues of *Ms.*

This publication is made possible, in part, by public funds from the New
York State Council on the Arts.

Photographs: On the cover (clockwise): Cora Tucker and her mother; Greenham
Common women (Paula Allen); Gale Cincotta (Steve Kagan). Interior: p. 3, Marie
Cirillo; p. 17, Bernice Kaczynski (Sandy Livingston); p. 37, Gale Cincotta (Steve Ka-
gan); p. 57, (left) Maria Fava and (right) Mildred Tudy (Marcus Bonisson); p. 75. Mary
Sinclair (*Midland Daily News*); p. 89, Cathy Hinds (Merry Farnum); p. 107, Alice
Weinstein and Marion Weisfelner (Esther Zanville); p. 119, Cora Tucker; p. 133, Green-
ham Common women, (center) Simone Wilkinson (Paula Allen).

*For my parents, with love, immense pride in them,
and gratitude every day for the values they gave us*

Contents

Foreword

This is a book about a most important kind of work. There is more need for this work in our country than there are people to perform it. There are few barriers to entry, and there is lots of on-the-job training. Compared to the contributions of these labors, there are few awards or expressions of gratitude. Yet without such efforts over the years, we would be living in an authoritarian society marked by an autocratic government and oligarchic economy far beyond our contemporary jeremiads.

I am referring to the citizen work that provides the firmament of our democracy—the unsung initiatives of deeply caring people. The process of becoming an active citizen does not start with the particular provocation of a perceived injustice. There is something in the upbringing and personal culture of an individual that provides the necessary receptivity to activism. It is a combination of personal dignity, compassion for others, a welling of self-confidence in the absence of anyone else to rely on, and dynamic preservation instincts covering family, community, and principles of fairness.

In these portraits of women working at their citizenship, Anne Witte Garland describes qualities of life that are beyond conventional ambitions. In seeking justice, these heroic individuals combine spiritual reserves with pragmatic applications. They are not content with just espousing abstract righteous paths; they take on malignant powers and faceless bureaucracies. While others make their living with little regard for consequences, these women are making life worth living for themselves and for their neighbors. The personal growth that comes with striving for social well-being is one of the more fascinating dimensions of these women's stories.

Overall, this volume exudes motivation for the reader and raises interesting questions: Why are most community activists women— does their gender influence their activism? What would happen if there were no one preserving and defending the community, which defines the genuine richness and justice of a society? How long can we continue to define work (and thereby status) only as something one does at a workplace for remuneration, mostly for employers?

In a redefinition of work, there can arise the redirection of our society's priorities—from one of immersion in *means* that lead to troubling *ends,* to one in which *ends* discipline *means* toward a more humane and productive society. Anne Witte Garland's book is a narrative with vaulting horizons that etches the potential for women to expand the frontiers of justice.

Ralph Nader

Preface

We have all, at one time or another, experienced a sense of rage at our powerlessness to change some injustice inflicted on us or on others. The feeling may be triggered by something as simple as a badly timed rent or utility bill increase, or as forceful and basic as the nuclear threat looming over us. I wrote this book in order to tell the stories of women who have turned powerlessness and rage into constructive action.

The fourteen women in this book are very unusual because of the way they live by their convictions. When I started this project, I deliberately sought out women who became activists for personal, practical reasons. Not just because they were raised that way, or because they felt abstractly that it was the "right" thing to do, but because they'd been personally faced with a threat or sense of injustice, and squarely faced it down. I've always been moved by such stories. I think they're inspiring and hopeful, and they bear telling because of their personal significance and their significance for democracy. As electoral politics seems to have less and less meaning for people, the kind of hands-on politics that these women activists engage in becomes increasingly important.

People have asked me why I singled out women as the subjects for this book. The answer is straightforward: Although there are plenty of men today who are bucking the system and putting themselves on the line because of their ideals, there are many more women who are doing that. The leadership and ranks of community groups are predominately women. Women are the vocal, passionate leaders in fights against toxic waste dumps, against nuclear power, and against nuclear weapons. There are many theories for why this is so, and I'm not sure that any one theory is satisfactory. I did make a point of raising the question with the women I interviewed, their friends, and professionals who study social movements. Some speculated that since women are traditionally concerned with home and family and community, they're the first to recognize threats to them and to act on those threats. Other people argued that men are more integrated into the system that creates the threats, and that since women have been excluded from that system historically, they have less to lose than men in fighting it. I was also told that women can get angry more easily than men, and are more easily moved to fight back; on the other hand, I was told that women are conditioned to be mediators, so they're naturals for activist work.

Although I do try to explore what motivates the women in this book, I didn't undertake to write a scholarly or psychological work. I wanted to tell these women's stories, get across a feeling for their personalities, and describe the problems that sparked their activism, the obstacles they've encountered, and how they've met challenges and setbacks. The women in this book come from a variety of social and ethnic backgrounds and have taken on widely diverse problems. But they're also very similar to one another, in that for the most part their approaches to activism are intuitive, not trained.

Writing the book has been a very special experience. The first interview I conducted was with Marie Cirillo, who, like several others in the book, shared her home with me while I plied her with questions about what she does and why she does it. I had to take Marie's word that in other seasons the Appalachian landscape is beautiful; it was the middle of winter when I arrived there, and the scene of poverty and environmental damage from coal strip mining was particularly bleak. Marie, like most of these women, has periodically faced harassment because of her work. While I was there she received threatening phone calls, and her friends were concerned about her safety. The last night I spent at her house we stayed up talking about fear and courage.

When I drove away alone the next morning, the landscape was transformed with fresh snow that covered up any evidence of strip mining or poverty. Only one car had traveled before me on the small mountain road from Marie's house; snow covered the road and clung to the trees, and icicles had formed on branches and on the rocky roadside. I was overwhelmed by the spectacular beauty of it, beauty that was heightened because of the powerful, lingering experience of Marie's idealism, and because I understood her love for the place and her commitment to the community there.

That summer, I was driving in England with Simone Wilkinson, who was telling me about the despair she had felt about nuclear weapons before she became involved with the Greenham Common peace movement. At the time she first learned of Greenham and visited the peace camp there, she had a job as a sales representative for medical equipment, which involved a lot of travel by car. It was a harsh winter, with unusually heavy snow. Simone described very eloquently to me how exquisite and fragile nature seemed to her that season as she drove around the English countryside, and how her experience of it was all the stronger because of her newly found hope through her peace activism that nature and people might not be destroyed. I was again drawn in to the intensity with which these women seem to live, and the fullness of their lives that can be both difficult and exhilarating. I hope that this book conveys some of that fullness.

I thank all the women in this book—both for the work they are doing, and for sharing their time and experiences so generously with me. I'm also very grateful to Ralph Nader, who made the project possible, and to John Richard and Jean Highland, who gave me their enthusiasm and support. My colleagues and former colleagues at the Fund for Public Interest Research and the New York Public Interest Research Group were generous in giving me leaves to work on this project; they are dedicated and wonderful to work with. Essential Information, Inc. provided financial assistance at a crucial time. Joanne O'Hare and The Feminist Press have been the kind of editor and publisher a writer usually can only wish for—supportive, patient, and convinced of the value of the book. Joanne Edgar and *Ms.* magazine have provided a much-appreciated outlet for my writing, including adaptations of material from two of these chapters. I also thank Joan Holt for her efforts to shut down the Indian Point nuclear power plant, and for her friendship. My sisters and brothers and their families constantly give me close friendship, inspiration, and joy. David Garland listens to me, helps me, reads every word I write, and offers very useful suggestions. I don't always accept them graciously, but they—and he—are extremely important to me.

Anne Witte Garland

Introduction

The title Anne Witte Garland has chosen for her book, *Women Activists,* is as deceptively simple as the task she has set for herself: telling the stories of women who have found themselves engaged in what, for lack of better words, we call political or community activism. It is clear that the women whose lives form the basis of Garland's text see their political lives and commitments as simple, and in many cases as natural to them as breathing. Some readers may be so taken with the simplicity of the stories, and with their straightforward telling (often in the words of the women themselves), that they too will come to see the book, and the lives it attempts to portray, as simple. There is much to be learned from this sort of reading of the book, and it has great charm. By themselves, the charm and the learning more than justify the considerable effort that Garland has invested in her research and writing, and by themselves they will amply reward even the casual reader. Underneath the simple veneer, however, lies a splendid complexity, a tapestry of themes woven into a sum far more complicated and significant than its surface parts.

Each of the stories in the book stands comfortably alone, both as a story in the literary sense, and as a testament to the spirit of the woman or women who inhabit it. The tales are often far more dramatic than the tellers apparently believe them to be, for the subjects of these stories are particular women of our time—women who judge themselves "ordinary"; women not brought up to imagine themselves as leaders; women at first uneasy in the larger world, the one beyond their homes; women more accustomed to living with anger, pain, and despair than they are with channeling these into public action.

The question of how people become who they become, especially when they become activists, is one of the central themes that emerges from Garland's work. It is, however, by no means the only question the book raises. In each chapter, Garland is concerned with the roots of activism, both psychological and philosophical. She also considers the conditions under which activism becomes a necessary and essential response, certain conditions of interest to, say, political scientists and sociologists.

Each chapter also provides a particular history, not only of a particular woman, but of the issues that consume her. As often as not, that history contains important economic and political insights into the issues. What also emerges from these stories is a primer of organizing principles. As the women recount the stories of their involvement and the facts of their journeys, the similarities of the struggles become apparent. In discussing their strategies and tactics, their successes and failures, through what for them is often uncharted territory, the women activists provide a virtual handbook of organizing technique and method. The "handbook" speaks to questions of leadership as well as to organizing per se.

Finally—and importantly—there is feminism. The principals in this book are, after all, women. As women involved in battles ranging from auto safety through nuclear weapons, they have a good deal to say about the issues as well as about their roles as leaders. Their perspectives are informed by how the world treats them as citizens and as people. They are informed too by their own insights into what it means to be a woman engaged in late twentieth-century political action. Their experiences, perspectives, and insights will no doubt be of considerable interest to theorists and practitioners of feminism.

We will look briefly here at four issues dealt with in *Women Activists:* the roots of activism, certain conditions of activism, principles of political action, and feminism.

Roots of Activism

How people become who they become is a theme that is surely psychological in nature, but one that also possesses sociological and philosophical dimensions. Philosophical because each of these women speaks of the ways in which her activism has informed her sense of who she is, and of how her actions are grounded in dearly held principles of justice and equality. Sociological because activism is, by definition, social—it grows out of and acts on a fundamental understanding of the contexts of power and possibility. Because Garland encourages her subjects to explore not simply the facts of their activism, but also its roots, we are able to trace how women activists come into being.

In moments of high emotion, as well as in moments of stark rationality, these women activists point to anger as a principal motivator underlying their thinking and their behavior. Anger is often at the center of their tranformations from private actors in restricted universes to public leaders in universes encompassing all the important issues of the day. The anger comes, of course, from a variety of sources. And it crosses the putative barriers of age and racial differences; differences in education, background, and lifestyle; and differences in religious and political belief.

Gale Cincotta, who declined to allow her Chicago neighborhood to be exploited by real estate developers, claims that what motivated her most urgently was her anger. "When you look carefully at what's going on around you, you have to get angry. I got mad, and that gave me courage." What moved her to action, she says, was the steady unraveling of her belief that there was something wrong with her or something wrong with her children. Finally, she saw that the faults were not her own but rather that "there's something wrong with the system that has to be changed. When I first realized that, I got angry. And I've stayed angry." Gale's anger seems to sustain her as much as her hope and as much as her success.

Like Gale, Mildred Tudy is a community activist. Her history of involvement in the Williamsburg-Greenpoint neighborhood of Brooklyn spans more than twenty years. And like Gale, Mildred sees anger as an important force propelling her into action and sustaining her commitment. "Today, I get so angry sometimes because our country doesn't live up to that image [of a country of hope]. But in those [earlier] days I wasn't angry—I was bland. . . . I hadn't been troubled yet."

Cathy Hinds became angry when she recognized that a waste dumpsite was polluting her community's water supply. She was angrier still when she realized how little the government seemed to care. She has learned to express her anger with candor. "It makes me think that, damn it, this is *America,* this stuff shouldn't be happening." Cathy also discovered how to put her anger to work. "I'm not going to sit back and let it happen. I want to be part of fighting to do something about it."

Women activists find they have enough anger to sustain them over a lifetime of working for change. The anger must also be sufficient to overcome their fear in the face of harassment and ridicule. Bernice Kaczynski, known among her family and neighbors as a lamb, became angry when the city of Detroit and General Motors collaborated on a project that ultimately eradicated her entire neighborhood. "A lot of people asked me why I wasn't afraid. I'd be a damn fool to say I wasn't. . . . But I had enough anger in me to overcome the fear and go on fighting."

Anger overcomes fear, a common enough experience among activists. But fear also sometimes leads to despair. The four Greenham Common women whose words appear in Chapter 9 describe their feelings: "I had joined the peace movement out of sheer, total despair. . . . there was a tremendous sadness inside me." They speak of waking up with cold sweats, of having constant nuclear war nightmares, of deep and continuing depression. They are frightened for their lives and their children's lives. But their despair turns to hope when they discover they are not alone, and that there is action they can take. At Greenham Common, "I was witnessing the creativity of women. . . . And what they were doing there was so clearcut and simple—just being there, a constant presence . . . That simplicity was the joy of Greenham, that and finding others who felt as intensely as I did, and who were dealing with their fear so directly."

The antidote the Greenham women found for their despair is the same antidote Cathy Hinds, Mildred Tudy, and Bernice Kaczynski (as well as others in this book) found for their anger. A commitment to change and to being part of the change. It all comes down to what virtually every woman activist in this book says, in one form or another: "I had to do something."

The fear that brought the Greenham women together, the fear that they dispelled through concerted action, is as instantly, humanly recognizable as the anger that appears to motivate many activists. The anger and the despair come from the perception that they do not control their own lives and that they are considered powerless. The epiphanies come when they begin to empower themselves and begin to take control. An observer of Bernice's Poletown action says it well:

> The women went through all the stages everyone else went through—
> the same shock, and denial, and depression. But they were astute; they
> never lost sight of the fact that their rights were being violated. . . .
> They were the first to recognize the injustice . . . they know simply that
> what was happening stunk.

This recognition that something is radically wrong, that something is terribly unjust, that something downright stinks, runs throughout the stories of these "ordinary" women. The odor is too strong for them to bear.

Certain Conditions of Activism

What is most striking about the women activists whose stories make up this book is that, in many instances, the women find themselves at first very much alone. Alone in their identification of a problem, alone in the intensity with which they believe the problem to be important, and alone in their obsession to do something about it. It is as though they were initially hurled into a vacuum—with no allies, guideposts, directions, or set of instructions, and often without the sure sense that they are right.

Consider Mary Sinclair. Her early, benign, scientific interest in nuclear power led her into serious apostasy—a falling from her abiding faith in technology. Her first efforts were aimed at basic information gathering; she wished only to be well informed. The hostile reaction she received surprised her. Labeled a maverick, a troublemaker, a "know-nothing housewife," Mary was ostracized by her community and her church. For years she waged a one-woman campaign—at first to gather and disseminate information, and only later, as her confidence in herself and her judgments about nuclear power grew, to oppose the building of a nuclear power plant in her Michigan community. As information about the reality of nuclear power became public—a direct result of Mary's untiring efforts—the number of mavericks grew. In 1984, when Mary was sixty-five with seventeen years of her campaign behind her, the nuclear power plant was finally prohibited from opening for business. As someone says of another activist in the book, in a statement appropriate to all of them, Mary is able to do what she does because she's "got guts. There's just nothing else to it but courage."

Consider also the "Audi ladies" of Long Island, Alice Weinstein and Marion Weisfelner—women who refused, against all odds, to accept a corporation's accusations of bad driving and a community labeling them troublemaking, middle-aged Jewish bitches. Like Mary Sinclair, operating in a vacuum and completely inexperienced in matters of dissent, Alice and Marion formed an Audi Victims Network, found consumer agencies, filed complaints, and pressured the Audi Corporation to recall the defective automobiles.

Cathy Hinds also operated in a vacuum, finding courage and strength she didn't know she had to ask questions and to demand action. Gale Cincotta says it is simply a matter of taking responsibility when all others refuse. All of the women in the book face bleak moments when they believe there is nowhere to turn, when they cannot comfort themselves with the hope that someone else will fight this fight, or that somehow things will turn out all right. At these moments they must decide—almost literally—to blaze new trails. It may be argued that the idea of a vacuum is itself a critical factor in developing activism. The stories of these women suggest that while the presence of a vacuum may not create activism, it adds essential urgency to the cause of the activist.

Principles of Political Action

It all begins with talk. As health officials say about women like Cathy Hinds, "Often the first alert of hazardous waste pollution in a community was through women talking among themselves about reproductive or other health problems."

It also began with talking for Alice Weinstein, the original "Audi lady." "She got on the phone, and within hours she had the names of five people whose Audis had shot out of control in the same way." Listening is essential, amends Marie Cirillo, who spent years prying out of her Appalachian community the subjects of their real concern.

According to the women of this book, identifying the problem and its causes is the first step toward activism. After talking and listening comes education—educating oneself and the community about the issues. Becoming expert and establishing credibility are closely associated with this process, and they become foundations for action. Disillusionment with government and other institutions that women expect will act in their behalf is targeted as a necessary part of the process that transforms docile, concerned citizens into political activists. Making connections, finding allies, and creating coalitions are bulwarks of activism; the way the women of this book trudge through these trenches is described in each chapter.

The principles of action emerging from this work are both simple and profound. "Active presence" is a necessary ingredient for all the movements mentioned—from Cora Tucker's predictable presence at every supervisors' meeting in her Virginia county to the Greenham Women's encampment. Slow and cautious beginnings are best, they argue; begin with little crusades. Gale Cincotta: "People are always saying you can't do it. But maybe you *can.* You can do a piece of it. At least you can build a base for someone else to build on. . . . What we have is people power. Other people have money power or 'political' power. We've got to fight with our people power." Cora Tucker speaks directly to those who wonder exactly when the conditions are ripe for action: "The time doesn't *get* right; you make it right."

Mary Sinclair knows what it means to sustain a commitment over time, and she says the most important thing is to "avoid becoming bitter." Others say activists can never be too skeptical, but they must never be cynical. Learn to interpret gains gradually, they say, and practice infinite patience. Recognize that the process of change is painstakingly slow, but know that "all it takes for community change to happen is for someone to pull people together to do things for themselves."

The chapters are rich with these sorts of general observations on how political action is initiated and maintained. They are also replete with specific details on using the press, on door-to-door activity, on letter-writing campaigns (Cora Tucker took supplies to local beauty parlors so that women under dryers could write their government representatives), on mounting public demonstrations, and on how not to accept the unacceptable.

Feminism

Finally, we look at the issue of feminism as it reveals itself in this book. Whatever the issue, wherever the battlefield, it is agreed that women are at the center of movements for change. On nuclear power: "Citizens' groups were forming around the country on the issue, with many of the efforts being led by women." In Poletown: "The most committed and energetic opponents of the city and General Motors were women." On toxic waste: "There are maybe a couple hundred people around the country—largely women—whose response has been to turn the pain and anger and fear into a very constructive working for solutions." In Chicago: "What I found was that most of the people who got involved in community organizations *were* women."

It is difficult to evade the question of why, time and again, it is women who populate movements. The women of the book often speculate on differences they see between women and men that account for greater female participation. In Appalachia, Marie Cirillo guesses that it is easier for women to learn and grow, while their men exhaust themselves in the mines. "It's the women who are most involved with nurturing in the community as well as in the family." In Poletown, one woman argues that "women are more aggressive, really. I think we find it more natural to go out and fight for what we think is right. I think the men, a lot of the time, just let it go. They figure it's a lost cause. But that's not the attitude to take."

The women also speculate on their own brands of feminism. Maria Fava didn't think she was a feminist. "But when I have to fight for my children, I do. And I guess I've always been a feminist in my own way; I've always fought for what I think is important. To me that's what it means to be a feminist—being able to fight for your rights, your community, your children, and other women."

Mary Sinclair says feminism became real to her when she recognized that "my freedom of speech [is] as important to me as my concerns about nuclear power." Cora Tucker remembers her high school teacher admonishing her, "Nobody can make you a second-class citizen but you. You should always be involved in what's going on around you." Almost all the women activists tell stories of empowerment—moments in which they became, in Helen John's terms, "emboldened." Their senses of themselves as people and as women changed.

Many of the women activists are mothers, and many of them link together nurturance-activism-feminism. Echoing Marie Cirillo's remark about women and nurturing in the community, Mary Sinclair says, "I started seeing the nuclear issue in terms of [my children]." She and her husband "both felt this work of mine was just another part of parenting our children." A woman who works with Gale Cincotta says that the women involved in their Chicago community organization "carried those concerns about their home and family a step further, into the community."

The ability of these women to make connections between their families, their communities, and the world outside is a strength. Gale says, "The way my mind works, it all fits together. . . . weaving back and forth from one issue to another . . . how they're related. But that's the kind of thinking that's missing in Washington." Marie Cirillo has a point of view she attributes to her love of mountain terrain, but it also represents the way many feminists view the world:

> When you drive around in flat country, you have a certain perspective of things—of the land, for instance, or trees. But when you drive around in the mountains, at one point you're looking at the base of a tree, another moment at the top of a tree. You see all angles of the physical things around you, and I think that gives you the capacity to see certain angles of life that other people don't see. I believe that mountain people have something that other people don't have, and should have. They know that human life is sustained by natural life, and that what comes from the air and soil is the stuff that we all live on. These things are life sources; they have a breath and living force behind them.

Whether the issue is nuclear power or nuclear weapons, education, toxic waste, auto safety, or the quality of neighborhood community life, these women persist in the perception that "everything is connected" and that their actions are natural extensions of their nurturing or parenting role.

The tenets of connectedness and what Marie Cirillo calls "the angles of life," a perspective on the natural world, are the foundation of what some have called a new sort of feminism, a feminism that rests on the twin assumptions that everything is connected and that the historic and constructive role of women has been nurturance, while the historic and dangerous role of men has been conquest. This new feminism, or "ecofeminism" as it is sometimes called, suggests nothing less than that the survival of the earth is dependent on feminists—female and male feminists—who commit themselves to nurturance rather than conquest. The women activists in this book, whether they specifically articulate ecofeminism or not, seem to be apostles and spokeswomen of this evolving feminism. And the men who join them and speak about them seem decidedly to understand.

Women Activists invites us to enter into the worlds of particular women engaged in particular commitments, and it invites us to ask and attempt to answer for ourselves the questions their stories raise. It also provides us with several prisms through which to view the world of activism: our own, those of the women who generously share their stories, and those of the people who join or observe them. It is through the multiplicity of these views, and the collected experiences of epiphany, action, victory, or defeat, in understanding the statement, "I had to do something," that we find ourselves moving toward some kind of truth. Truth is what this book is finally about, and why it seems simple but cannot be.

Frances T. Farenthold

Community
and
Neighborhood

"Every Mountain Hollow"

Marie Cirillo

1

"What attracted me here in the first place were the problems, and what's kept me going is the drive to understand what people can do about their problems. One thing I've learned is that every mountain hollow in Appalachia has people capable of doing what people here have done."

*I*n little ways, the curving mountain roads where Marie Cirillo lives in northeastern Tennessee, near the Kentucky border, reveal a story of Appalachia. Trailer homes and simple houses built by the people living in them are scattered up and down the hollows, the narrow areas between mountains. In the winter, gray smoke rises out of chimneys, from the wood-burning stoves that heat the homes. In the summer, vegetable gardens next to the houses provide people with meals. Thickets and trees on the side of a road occasionally give way to imposing views of mountains that have been gashed and skinned by strip-mining for coal.

Land and the coal that lies under it are the only wealth in this area of the mountains, with all but the smallest portion of the land owned and controlled by a few corporations. Land, accordingly, has become something of an obsession for Marie; it goes hand-in-hand with her other longtime obsession, that of helping to build and sustain a community. To Marie, control of the land is at the crux of the problem faced by the people in Appalachia who are trying to gain control over their own lives.

The heart of Appalachia, where Marie settled and has worked for twenty years as a "community developer," as she calls it, is far from Brooklyn, New York, where she was born in 1929. But to Marie, the transition was completely natural. A small, trim woman, dressed typically in slacks and a turtleneck or a delicately flowered shirt, with short brown hair that she cuts herself, Marie looks perfectly comfortable with the rural life she's chosen.

Growing up in Brooklyn, the daughter of music teachers, she spent summers with her grandparents in rural Kentucky. Early on she developed an appreciation of the differences between urban and rural life. "The population in the town where my grandparents lived was two hundred or three hundred people; my grandfather milked the cows and we fed the chickens and worked in the garden. But more important, what I saw there that I didn't see back home in Brooklyn—and I knew even then that I liked it—was the close interaction of people, not just with the land but with one another. My grandfather had been the mayor and he worked at the bank; people were always coming to him and asking him things. It was a more direct way of living—people did things for themselves; if someone's place was burning, everyone cooperated and knew just what to do. Back in Brooklyn, when I saw a fire truck speeding down the street, or when we put trash out to be whisked away somewhere, I realized I had no idea of how things happen in the city!"

Marie was already being drawn to the vision of community that has inspired her entire career. "My father's mother was still living in a little Italian ghetto in New York, in the area where my father had been raised. On Sundays during the year, I'd go visit her. Even that ghetto atmosphere seemed somehow friendlier than our suburban-like section of Brooklyn. Kids would be out sitting on the stoops, and people would be talking to each other from their windows, just passing the time of day."

There was another strong influence at work on Marie as well—the Catholic church. She was raised Catholic, attended Catholic elementary and high schools, and had relatives in Kentucky who were nuns and priests. As early as grade school, Marie had made up her mind to be a nun. "My attraction had to do with the fact that I admired the Sisters who taught in the school, but when I heard them talk about the lives of the saints, or about good deeds, I wondered why I didn't see them actively doing more of that sort of thing themselves—taking people in from the street, taking care of the poor or the sick." Marie wanted to be a missionary. She was attracted at first to the Maryknoll order, which did foreign mission work, but when she was in high school she heard about a new order, formed to do home mission work chiefly in the rural South. "It all seemed so worthwhile—even romantic," she recalls. A year out of high school, in 1949, she became the twelfth woman to join the Glenmary Home Mission Sisters.

But it wasn't all romance. Being a nun back then meant obeying superiors' orders. "They asked me which I preferred, nursing or teaching—I said neither, but if I had to choose, it would be nursing. So they made me teach." Marie was sent to take education courses, and then to rural Kentucky to teach for a year in a two-room school— "probably the most unhappy year of my life." She then got her first taste of mission work, with stints in several Appalachian communities, and loved it. Eventually she was assigned to be cook for forty men at the Glenmary seminary; since she enjoys cooking, the job seemed challenging at first, but its appeal wore off quickly. "I would hear bits and pieces about the men's approach to mission work, filtering into the kitchen. I spent a lot of time thinking about what I would do if I were out in the missions, and began to think that I probably had better ideas than some of them did. That was way before I was conscious of any women's movement—I just thought I could probably do things better."

Ironically, it was in uptown Chicago, where she finished her undergraduate degree in sociology, that Marie came into contact again with Appalachian culture, while conducting field work in the considerable Appalachian community that had migrated to city ghettos to look for jobs. The displaced mountain people trying to survive in the city made a lasting impression on her.

By this time, there was a growing split within the Glenmary order. The root of the trouble was tension over what Marie calls "an emerging new spirituality." The Catholic church in general was being rocked by Vatican Council II, which was an attempt to redefine the church's role in modern times, and was leading to challenges of its more traditional, authoritarian ways. "It was a time of rethinking and renewal," says Marie. Women were studying and teaching theology for the first time, for instance, with the result that women theologians were challenging the bastion of male theologians. "It began to come down to a question of who we'd be loyal to, our Sisters or the men, and it didn't seem to make sense to hold on to loyalties to the men when we were part of a women's community."

The nuns' experiences in the missions fueled their discontent. "Out in the missions, we just couldn't conform to conditions that most nuns could conform to, and were supposed to conform to, according to the laws of the church back then. There were issues of when you had to be in at night, whom you could go around with, even the areas of the house that were supposed to be cloistered. Laypeople weren't allowed to see Sisters' dining rooms. Well, if you lived in a house and local people came in and weren't able to see your dining room, they'd wonder what was going on! And when you're trying to organize adults and have to be home at nightfall, you're obviously not going to get very far."

There were other problems, too. When Marie and other women joined the convent, part of the attraction was the community life they'd share. To create that community out in the missions, the aim was to have at least four nuns living together. The priests in the missions wanted the nuns' help in running their churches and schools, but one church couldn't economically sustain four nuns, since there were often only about thirty parishioners. "The priests solved the problem by going around to the local churches and asking them to 'buy in' to support us. But then we had to deliver the services—which meant traveling and traveling to all these little Catholic churches, with parishioners who were relatively well off. Meanwhile, there wasn't time to minister to the poor people who really needed us."

After working in those conditions, the nuns began to develop their own ideas about how they could work more effectively. For one thing, they saw that rural communities desperately needed medical care, and that some of them could serve a useful function by practicing as nurses. But in those days, most public health agencies weren't going to hire a woman who wore a habit and veil and looked, as Marie puts it, like a Catholic preacher. That led Marie and others to consider wearing lay clothes, well before most nuns in other orders were toying with the idea.

The bishop of Cincinnati at the time, under whose jurisdiction the Glenmary order fell, felt responsible for seeing that the nuns conformed with church law, and asserted his authority. "It had us in a bind. We found we couldn't take the next steps, couldn't do the very things that we had discovered we *had* to do to be effective in our work. For me the last straw was when the bishop appointed a Franciscan priest to deal more directly with us, to interview each of the Sisters and get a better sense of the problems. I told our superior that if the priest would go out in the missions to learn about them firsthand before meeting with us, I'd talk to him, but that if he didn't, I wasn't going to talk to him—he didn't, and I didn't."

In 1966, forty women left the order individually. The following year, a group of forty-four more women, including Marie, left the order—but not before restating their commitment to continuing rural community work.

Marie found herself haunted by the question of why so many Appalachian people were forced to leave their home and move to cities. "Many of the people I worked with in Chicago were intensely unhappy in the city; they'd only moved there because they were starving back at home. It was very different from what my sociology textbooks portrayed. The message I got from the textbooks was that the pride of America was its great urban centers, and that although people all over were catching on, the Appalachian people were among the last—

though, by golly, even they were finally catching on and moving to the cities." When she left the convent, Marie set out to find an Appalachian community that suffered from outmigration. She reasoned that if she stayed in one community long enough, she would be able to identify the causes for the migration and help people to start tackling them.

Federal government antipoverty programs were in their heyday then, and federal aid was filtering into the isolated mountain communities. Through a man associated with the federal programs, Marie heard about the town of Clairfield, Tennessee. It was a coal mining community, but in the 1940s underground coal mining had largely given way to strip mining, which was less labor intensive and cost most of the men their jobs—and even their homes. When coal companies left the area, they left only the environmental damage behind, often burning the company housing that they had put up for workers and their families. Public services were virtually nonexistent, and most people who remained in the area lived below the poverty level. The population of the community had once been 12,000; by 1967 it had dwindled to 1,200.

Marie decided to settle there, and moved into an apartment attached to the post office, in a building that had once been a coal company commissary. Jean Luce, a friend of Marie's who had also left the Glenmary order, joined her, taking a job with the county-administered federal poverty program, funded by the Office of Economic Opportunity. Marie approached the Catholic bishop in Nashville for support; to his credit, he recognized the value of what she was proposing, and the diocese hired her to work as a community organizer. (The diocese has continued to pay her a small salary and to provide modest funds to use as seed money for community projects.)

Through her experiences in the convent and missions, Marie had already acquired a wealth of knowledge about community programs, government agencies, and funding. It was now a matter of trying out what she knew, to see what would work and what wouldn't in her new situation. The postmistress is often a quiet leader and instinctive organizer in a rural community; Clairfield's postmistress, Louise Adams, became Marie's close friend and mentor. From her, Marie gained invaluable insights into the mountain communities and the people living in them. "In the early days, I would hold meetings and they wouldn't go at all the way I'd expected. I'd go to Louise, and she'd carefully explain to me what I'd done wrong. The next time, things would be better."

The year before Marie and Jean arrived in Clairfield, a Quaker volunteer had lived there, and with his help the people in the community had chosen an old school house to turn into a community center. Renovations were begun on the building, and Jean, whose job involved directing the center, called meetings to start discussing projects to undertake. Marie saw as her own first task simply listening to the needs of the people. She quickly learned what wouldn't work; at one point, after hearing people's complaints about things like food stamps and inadequate health care, she suggested that several local people go with her to Nashville and meet with some government agencies. "We piled into my station wagon and went around to different offices with our problems—with no results," she says. "Louise later told me that she had never expected the agencies to be of any help."

The community's first success was setting up a health clinic, sorely needed because of inadequate or nonexistent health care in an area where many of the men were suffering from black lung and other diseases from mining. Marie helped to track down medical volunteers, and encouraged the clinic's board to incorporate as a nonprofit organization, which would make it easier to get funding and—very importantly—to survive independently of the government. The clinic was opened in 1968; for the local people, it was just a first taste of what they could accomplish together.

It was clear by now what Marie and the local people were striving for: forming and running local organizations to meet the needs of people in the area, while serving as realistic models for other communities. The target area encompassed the several small, unincorporated towns in the valley around Clairfield, bordered on either side by the Pine and Cumberland mountains; Louise Adams proposed using the name "Model Valley." The name stuck, and the latest project became the Model Valley Economic Development Council.

It soon became obvious that incorporating as independent organizations was a good move. About a year and a half after Marie and Jean arrived in Clairfield, key changes were made in the government's poverty program that resulted in less local control by poor people themselves over the federally funded projects. Some county officials, who didn't like the center's tampering with the status quo, started pressuring Jean to change the focus of her work; instead she opted to quit her job and leave the area. The same officials probably assumed—and hoped—that Marie would leave as well, but she had something very different in mind. She loved the mountain communities, had gained the trust of many of the local people, and was as determined as ever to help them identify and start grappling with the fundamental problems plaguing their area.

With the changes, the community center lost its vitality and effectiveness, and the board of the health clinic decided that, if the clinic was to succeed, it should be disassociated from the community center. "The health clinic had resources, it had volunteers, it had everything but a building to function in," says Marie. "But when they started looking for land so that they could build a new place, they were stymied." That was just the first of what would be a series of frustrating attempts to find land for the community organizations, and it was an indication of the extent of the stranglehold on the community by the corporations that owned the land.

The Model Valley Economic Development Council achieved an important breakthrough, then, when it was able to buy thirty acres of land in Clairfield from a local family. The first thing to go up on the land was a new building for the health clinic. Clinics were started up in nearby towns in the valley as well, many with funding from the federal Appalachian Regional Commission and with the help of energetic volunteers from Vanderbilt University. The community was to experience the inevitable false starts and obstacles, though. In 1970, the economic development council obtained a federal small business loan to start up its own company, a factory for assembling wooden loading pallets. The choice of business made sense: The area had abundant timber that statistics showed was underutilized, job training would be relatively easy, and an out-of-state company had promised an ample market for the product. The factory began operation the following year, but never reached more than 60 percent of capacity, with fifteen employees. It folded in three years, in part because the landowning corporations wouldn't give the new company access to land to cut timber.

Other projects were under way, including the Model Valley Craft Group, and Tilda Kemplen's day care center. Tilda, a school teacher, had been one of the first local people to attend the early meetings at the Clairfield community center. After several meetings she went up to Marie and said, "I've been watching you and listening to what you're saying about starting organizations, and the one thing I really want to work on is day care. So I'm going to start up a day care center."

The first year, Tilda got children together for activities outside under trees. Then she got a trailer, a neighbor gave her a place to put it, and she started her day care center. She applied for and received some federal educational funding, and after several moves was finally able to buy a little piece of land with a building, which houses a greenhouse, a used clothing store, and a library as well.

"One thing I've got in my favor—the thing a lot of people here don't have—is self-confidence," Tilda says. "I think that comes from my family, from the way I was brought up. So I guess I just took the bull by the horns, and went at it. When I started to teach in the rural schools, I saw all those children who came back to the mountains from Chicago or Detroit or Cincinnati—sometimes they'd be in the school a week and they'd move back to the city. It upset me awfully, because you couldn't do much for those children. Nobody could. They were torn apart, uprooted. And adults, too. I've worked with so many people who just don't believe they can do anything. I've spent a good deal of my time with women—staff people and mothers of the children—trying to help them understand that they're worth something, that what they've got to say is important. I try to instill that in the children, too. And then I see them just blossoming out—it's like a rosebud to begin with, and all of a sudden I see them blossoming into a rose.

"And Marie's role here, the way I see it, has been to help that to happen—to help people to help themselves, help them get together groups and to take control of their own lives and community. She's shown people ways to do what they want. She's also brought stability, by staying here so long. She didn't just come in one year, get a big salary, and go back to write a book about it or something—meanwhile leaving people the same as before or even worse off. I've seen the way some churches have operated here, starting up settlements with schools and things, and then falling by the wayside because the community people had no input into it. The church might be the 'good samaritan,' bringing in people, building a place, giving the local people handouts. But then they'd leave, and everything would be gone— they'd even tear down the building.

"With Marie it's the other way around. She has helped groups to become aware of their own talents, their rights, and all the things they can do for themselves. So even if she had to leave tomorrow for some reason, the groups would still be able to function; it would be a better place because she'd been here."

Marie has continued to live alone. In 1969, she moved into a little house up in a hollow—a comfortable, inviting house with a porch, a woodburning stove, and a tiny kitchen where she often bakes bread or cooks meals for gatherings at her house. A poster in her study reads, "Pray for the dead—fight like hell for the living," a quote from an early organizer of coal miners, Mary Harris Jones (who was known as "Mother Jones"). A cross in Marie's living room is from her days in the convent novitiate, and she has pieces of pottery made by another former Glenmary nun. (Most of the women who left the order together have stayed in touch, through an organization Marie encouraged them to form to support them in their commitment to live and work in rural communities.) When volunteers or other outsiders come to the area, they usually stay at Marie's house.

Marie sees an important part of her work to be that of building connections between the community and the outside world. Not the way she perceives some federal government programs to have attempted it—"to tie Appalachia into the rest of the country, to make the people and places conform to other people and places in the mainstream"—but to enable local people to tap outside resources, and even more, to understand the parallels between Appalachia and other parts of the world. "Louise Adams once said something to me that pleased me; she said that after she had known me for a few years, she had a totally different perspective on the world, that it made her see her own community differently." Marie sometimes brings in films to show to local people, on such issues as land control in Central America, and they're taken aback by how similar the problems are to Appalachia's. She is on the board, and served for a year as president, of Rural American Women, an organization based in Washington that serves as a network for women in rural communities, and she and Tilda once traveled to India to attend an international conference on strategies for rural women. Closer to home, she helped organize the Mountain Women's Exchange, a lively network of several groups in the area including crafts groups, Tilda's child care center, the "Home-Makers Construction Project," which trains women in home construction and rehabilitation, and Marie's latest project, the Community Land Association.

The Mountain Women's Exchange came about after Marie coordinated a conference in 1979 for Rural American Women, bringing together rural women's groups from all over the Southeast. "Whenever I go to events that seem a little extraneous to the immediate community here, I try to think about what I can get out of them that will be meaningful here," she says. "The conference had been this wonderful experience of just meeting other rural women, and it occurred to me that we had all these nonprofit groups nearby in Tennessee and Kentucky that had never made an effort to get together. I went to a couple of the women to see what they thought of having just a get-together at first. We set it up, and the dynamics of that group were amazing—you could hardly hear yourself talk for all the excitement and energy in the exchange that was going on. The group in Kentucky was so excited that there was a group here doing child care, because that was something they'd always wanted to do but didn't know how. They were all learning from one another—and the new group took off.

"In many ways, it seems there are more opportunities for women in Appalachia to grow than for the men. Even when the men have jobs to go to in the mines, there might be an hour to get to work, an hour back, and eight hours in the pits, with all their discomfort and risks—when they get home the men are ready to be babied. The woman does all the management of the home, and the care of the children—and her experience as a homemaker actually gives her much more opportunity to grow and learn, when you think of all the things she has to organize. And maybe it's women's instinct, but it's the women who are most involved with nurturing in the community as well as in the family. It's not a big splash; it's a slow, steady day-to-day thing, this growing process, but it's happening right here."

Another gradual process has been getting to the point where the community could deal directly and explicitly with what is probably the fundamental problem facing Appalachian communities, land control. "When I first moved here, it was before any of the educators and organizers in Appalachia were focusing on land problems. Early on I had heard the local people saying that the reason nothing could happen around here was that the companies owned all the land. But I didn't know what to do with that information; neither did they. When I went around saying, 'Well, what should we work on next?' of course no one said, 'Let's take over the land.' Instead, they mentioned things they thought they could achieve, like the health clinics, or even something as simple as getting together a little music group. But even the simplest things were difficult without a place for them."

While the groups struggled to find little pieces of land to build on, events in the region came together to focus new broad efforts on the land problem. When the health clinics were being formed, for instance, the students from Vanderbilt University who helped coordinate them started bringing in law students as well, to focus on other problems. Some of the students did a multicounty survey of land control in Appalachia and, since the findings showed that the interests controlling the land paid very little in taxes, an effort was organized to enforce state laws on land taxation. Out of that grew the organization

Save Our Cumberland Mountains (SOCM), which later worked to pass important legislation regulating strip mining.

SOCM had its share of enemies, chiefly the companies doing the strip mining, but also local people who were convinced by the companies that anti-strip-mining legislation would hurt the local economy. At one point the strip miners went to Washington to protest the new federal legislation that required companies both to apply for permission to do strip mining so that any potential harm to the environment and water supplies could be assessed, and to do some land reclamation work afterward to restore the mined sites to their previous condition. The strip miners asked local businesses to demonstrate their solidarity in opposition to the legislation by closing for a day, but the health clinic and development council refused to cooperate. Marie was harassed because of her support for SOCM (she was one of the founding members), and her stand on the strip-mining restrictions. Her house was shot at, and there were threats that she would be "burned out." She was out of town at the time of some of the worst threats, but a couple of organizers were staying at her house. Someone tampered with the steering wheel of her station wagon; the volunteer who was driving it had an accident, but wasn't hurt. When Marie got back, a friend met her at the airport and warned her not to go home. She ended up staying away for a week, until the worst of the hostility had died down.

One local man who has worked with Marie for years has an explanation for the trouble she has sometimes faced. "There used to be a lot of people under other people's thumbs here, and they're getting out; when that happens, there's bound to be a reaction. All it takes for community change to happen is for someone to pull people together to do things for themselves. Marie has been that guiding hand—she does what she does because of her background, her years in the convent. But Christians always get in trouble if they do what they're supposed to," he says.

Marie has moved on to a different way of dealing with the land issue, through a community land trust. The basic concept of a land trust is to accumulate property, not for individual ownership, but instead to be owned and managed democratically by a board, which determines how to put it to best use for the community. Marie has helped start both a regional and local land trust; within ten years, the Community Land Association in Clairfield has acquired sixty-six acres of land, mostly in small parcels from family owners. The land has been used for community and family gardens, for firewood and timber, and for housing. There are already several families living in their own homes, with long-term leases on land-trust land in Clairfield—families that probably wouldn't have their own homes if the land trust didn't exist. A "summer camp" has been built on one site, with a lodge and four cabins. For several weeks each summer, youth from Knoxville and other cities live together with mountain youth and work on such projects as learning how to do video documents of the local development activities, clearing land for pasture or garden sites, or stripping logs for log cabins.

As with other projects, the process of getting the land trust firmly established has been painstakingly slow. "We've come up against the problems of the 'system' more with the land trust than with any of the other groups," Marie says. A good deal of her time is spent dealing with bureaucracies—such as the IRS, which is reluctant to grant full nonprofit status to an organization that acquires and leases land, and the county government, which insists on registering the land trust land as a housing subdivision, bound by a whole set of inappropriate restrictions.

Part of what has sustained Marie through the long years of slow changes, starts and stops, and outright hostility has been her deep attraction to the mountains and rural people. "Anyone who has lived in mountains long enough knows that just the awesomeness and power of the earth above you and surrounding you does something to you; it humbles you in a way. It creates some response in your spirit that the flatlands, or the ocean, can't evoke.

"When you drive around in flat country, you have a certain perspective of things—of the land, for instance, or trees. But when you drive around in the mountains, at one point you're looking at the base of a tree, another moment at the top of a tree. You see all angles of the physical things around you, and I think that gives you the capacity to see certain angles of life that other people don't see. I believe that mountain people have something that other people don't have, and should have. They know that human life is sustained by natural life, and that what comes from the air and soil is the stuff that we all live on. These things are life sources; they have a breath and living force behind them. And I think that there are many urban people who have lost that connection, so that as a society we're lacking something. The nation is paying for it, I think, since we've lost the understanding that we depend on other forms of life for our own life. Living close to the land gives you a certain understanding of the universe—it makes you question more what life is all about.

"The mountain communities have faced cycles of major outside forces coming in and robbing them—there are other pockets of poverty in the country, but there probably isn't a larger chunk of land where there's been as much colonialism and exploitation of resources as here. First there was the timber industry, that helped to build up the East, then the coal industry. Then coal collapsed and people moved to cities in large numbers. With those cycles, people's community life changed. But there's a certain basic strength in the culture of the people and the land that has really survived all those changes, that hasn't been penetrated.

"When I first moved here, I was curious to see what would happen. I wondered—if I listened to the first thing that people wanted, and the second, and third, fourth, and fifth—whether I could begin to discern the components that go into making a community, what people would emerge to fill needs, and how long it would take until people dared to grapple with the thing that is the basic problem underlying all the others—the poor services, the joblessness. I've been here a long time now. Even those first groups we set up were confronted with problems of getting hold of land; it's taken us this long, and we still haven't succeeded—I know it's going to take a good while more. But what attracted me here in the first place were the problems, and what's kept me going is the drive to understand what people can do about their problems. One thing I've learned is that every mountain hollow in Appalachia has people capable of doing what people here have done."

"*The Human Element*"

Bernice Kaczynski

*"It turned out we were just the whatchacallit—the
'human element' is what they called us."*

*B*ernice Kaczynski collects dolls and knickknacks. Mostly gifts from her husband or children, they're displayed throughout her house: Shelves above the kitchen table hold dozens of tiny blown-glass animals; in the living room are dolls in fancy dresses, religious statues, and figurines—including a china Wonder Woman and frosted glass versions of Snow White and six of the seven dwarfs (one has gotten lost). Many of the figures are musical; sometimes the house settles a bit, triggering the music mechanisms so that they suddenly play a few notes and then are quiet again.

Bernice is an unlikely looking doll collector. She's in her mid-fifties, thin and just two inches over five feet tall, and full of energy. Her hair is cropped short, and she wears untucked shirts over blue jeans. She talks animatedly, and sprinkles her speech with expressions like "goddang" and "whatchacallit."

Bernice is also an unlikely person to have taken on the giant General Motors Corporation, but she did—along with many of her neighbors—for a bitter year and a half beginning in the summer of 1980. General Motors wanted to construct a new, modernized Cadillac factory, and offered to build in Detroit if the city would secure and clear about 500 acres of land for the project. City officials decided on a 465-acre area in east Detroit, an area that encompassed small businesses, churches, schools, and over a thousand homes—including Bernice's. Bernice and other residents wrote to officials, went to court, and took to the streets to protest. But in the end, with the enthusiastic cooperation of the city, state, and federal governments, General Motors prevailed, and Bernice spent several late summer nights in 1981 wrapping and packing her dolls and other belongings into boxes to move to another section of the city.

It wasn't the first time that General Motors's expansion plans had forced Bernice to move. Bernice was born in Hamtramck, a separate city in eastern Detroit. She never finished high school; she was married when she was sixteen to Harold Kaczynski, whose parents, like Bernice's, were Polish. Bernice had six children, three of them born at home. While the children were growing up, the couple rented houses. They had lived in one home in Hamtramck for twelve years when, in 1965, their landlord sold the property to General Motors, which leveled the house to add on to a parking lot for its nearby Chevrolet gear and axle plant. Bernice and Harry had no choice but to move. "When you rent, you always know that the house might be sold or the rent raised," Bernice says. "There was nothing we could do. We didn't even know what was happening until after the property had been sold. We were just given notice and told to move. It hurt, because it was a good place; I'd had the kids there, and they'd grown up there and went to school nearby. But we knew there's nothing you can do if the place doesn't belong to you."

So they looked for a new place to live, and finally found a house that they could rent with an option to buy, on Mitchell Street, in a Detroit area near Hamtramck. Bernice's mother had died, but her father was still living with her brother, who had a house close to Mitchell Street. He went to see the place Bernice was thinking of renting, and suggested that they buy it instead, so that no one could buy it out from under them. So with $500 from her father for a down payment, Bernice and Harry bought the house; it cost $4,500, and they didn't finish paying off the mortgage until early 1981, the year the City of Detroit forced them to move.

They quickly got to work fixing up the place. Harry, who was employed at the time doing maintenance for a downtown hotel, was adept at repairs. He replaced all the plumbing in the house, and lowered the ceilings and repaired walls and floors, working on one room at at time until he had it the way they wanted it. The idea was to eventually fix up the upstairs part of the house to rent out, or for one of the children to use with his or her own family. "It was a good solid house," says Bernice, "and with a little tender care it became home to us."

Meanwhile, they settled comfortably into the neighborhood. "Poletown," as the area became known, was actually a racially and ethnically mixed community, eventually with as many blacks as Poles, and with Albanians, Arabs, and Filipinos as well. Half of the 3,500 residents were older people, and almost 80 percent of them had incomes under $10,000 a year. Nevertheless, many people owned their own homes; the area was characterized by blocks and blocks of one-and two-family houses, mostly two-story wooden frames more than fifty years old. Many of the people living in them had been there all their lives, having inherited their homes from their parents.

"In Poletown you had everything to your heart's content," says Bernice. There was the transportation, for one thing: expressways close by, and for the older people without cars, convenient bus lines. Detroit residents are obsessed with and dependent on automobiles, but Bernice's neighborhood had unusually good public transportation. Near Bernice was a hospital, a drugstore, and grocery stores. The Chene and Trombley Market a few blocks away sold fresh meats and homemade Polish kielbasa sausage. South of the expressway, also within walking distance, was a market with fresh vegetables and live poultry. There had been some decline in the area over recent years, but residents considered it a solid community. There was a movement underway to attract urban renewal money for revitalizing the Chene Street shops. "It was a good neighborhood," says Bernice. "You could go anywhere and find streets with beautiful homes—old homes, but kept up. Sure you'd hit sections of maybe two or three blocks that weren't kept up. But you find that anywhere; usually it's the absentee landlords who don't keep up their places."

What meant the most to Bernice were her Poletown neighbors. Bernice's immediate block was integrated, and it was a tight-knit section. "People didn't look at you and say, 'That one's got lots of money,' or 'that one's on welfare.' No one cared if you were old or white or black. You were just part of the community. If you needed help—if your car broke down at six o'clock in the morning and your husband had to get to work—you knew the neighbors well enough to ring their doorbell and they'd come to the rescue. And if you were sick, people were more like they used to be when I was growing up; they were concerned about each other. Like the man next door—his daughter had died and he was alone, so we watched out for him. Every morning he'd be outside, puttering around; if he didn't come out, we worried about him and checked on him. And we used to watch out for each other's place when someone went on vacation.

"You can go into the suburbs, and some people don't even know who their neighbors are. In Poletown, you knew everybody. The people sat on porches; you walked down the street and saw your neighbors, who'd lived there for years, just like you. You'd always say, 'Hello, how are you today, how are the grandkids?' And it was the same for me when I'd sit on my porch; people would go by and say hello. In the stores, too, you knew the other people and chatted with them, and visited with the owners. You don't have that everywhere;

most places when you go to the store, you just pop in and out. You don't take time to be friendly."

Simple neighborly concerns were irrelevant to General Motors and the city, however. "It turned out we were just the whatchacallit—the 'human element' is what they called us," says Bernice.

The automobile manufacturer and city officials had other worries. After decades of producing large, inefficient automobiles, American carmakers suffered during the oil crisis of the 1970s. They had made a come back with record profits in 1978, but the 1979 Iranian revolution and resulting problems with oil supplies and prices made for another serious jolt. Detroit, where almost one out of every five jobs is connected with the auto industry, suffered along with the industry. In just one decade, over 100,000 auto and auto-related jobs were lost. The Chrysler Corporation had had a brush with bankruptcy and was still in trouble. In 1979 Chrysler closed its fifty-five-year-old Dodge Main plant in Hamtramck, which had employed almost 40,000 people in peak operation (including many of the Polish immigrants who lived in Bernice's neighborhood). GM had considered building a new plant in Detroit in the late 1970s, but its criteria for a suitable site couldn't be met, and the company built in Northern Ireland instead. A Uniroyal Tire plant had closed; Ford had built a tractor factory elsewhere, and GM had built an engine plant outside the city. By 1980, Detroit's unemployment rate was over 18 percent.

To save itself, the city was engaging in the kind of competitive tax giveaways that other midwestern and northeastern industrial cities had resorted to. The name of the game was trying to keep companies from closing plants and moving to states and countries with cheaper labor, fewer unions, and lower taxes—and Detroit's Mayor Coleman Young had made it clear he could play as aggressively as anyone.

General Motors, then the third wealthiest corporation in the world, was the only one of the "Big Three" American automakers whose future was secure in 1980. (Until 1980, GM hadn't shown an annual revenue loss since 1921.) In June 1980, the company responded to the auto industry slump by announcing a $40 billion, five-year program to modernize its plants and products, part of which called for closing two Detroit factories and replacing them with a single, sprawling, more efficient Cadillac plant, similar to a plant it had recently built in Oklahoma City. GM offered to stay in Detroit this time if the city would find and prepare a suitable site. Not about to miss this opportunity, the city eagerly commenced to do so. GM's criteria included a site large enough for the huge, one-story plant, power generating facilities, and parking; access to railroads and expressways; and, in order to keep to its May 1983 completion schedule, ready availability—much of the land would have to be cleared and titles to all the property involved would have to be in the city's hands in just one year.

The site the city chose included the old Chrysler Dodge Main plant in Hamtramck, which had been deeded to the city for one dollar the previous year, and which had the necessary road and railway access. Acquiring all the additional acreage wouldn't be as simple, but the residential area wasn't as densely populated as other sites the city had looked at, and, city officials reasoned, it was a slum anyway. They started applying for federal grants and loans to help pay for demolition work and for compensating and relocating the people involved.

Bernice and Harry were in North Carolina visiting one of their daughters that June when the news about the project broke. One week of their planned vacation was up. (Harry, who had been unemployed off and on since the downtown hotel had closed a few years earlier, was then working in a small factory.) Another daughter and son in Detroit called Bernice in North Carolina to tell her about a newspaper article that reported that their section of the city was to be sold and that the hospital had already agreed to move. At first Bernice wasn't alarmed. But then her son called back to say there *was* something to worry about—the city was acquiring the land for General Motors. Bernice and Harry thought it over and decided to cut their vacation short to go home and see for themselves what was going on.

They returned to a spate of community meetings. One of the first was a gathering of neighborhood people to discuss what was happening and what could be done to oppose it; the group formed the "Poletown Neighborhood Council" to fight the project. That kind of meeting was new to Bernice. "I had never belonged to any organization or anything," she says. "I just went along and listened to what people had to say because I was concerned. I had moved for GM before. This time, though, I was a homeowner—I had my rights to defend."

At the meeting, it was decided that flyers should be distributed informing residents about GM's plans. Carol Dockery, a young mother who lived across the street from Bernice, was put in charge of distribution, and Bernice helped out. She also continued to go to community meetings, which were marked by confusion and heated discussion about what was really happening, what the city's role was, and what rights the residents had. City representatives were on hand at some of the meetings to put forth the city's views and, since to them it was a foregone conclusion that they would prevail, to explain the relocation process.

"I got more and more involved, and angrier and angrier," Bernice says. "Sitting there at those meetings, I could just feel the city coming down on us. I was like everybody else, I didn't know exactly what my rights were. I just sat and listened at first. But then after a couple of meetings, someone was up there talking about moving and how the city would help us, and it hit me. I *knew* what moving was like; I didn't want to move. In Hamtramck I'd been a renter, but I knew what the homeowners went through. I could sense what it felt like for them to lose their houses. I had seen how people had renovated their homes and then were forced to leave them because of urban renewal. They were beautiful homes; the people had put in the kind of attention that people paid to their houses in Poletown, thinking, 'This is where I'm going to stay, and where I'm going to die, so before my husband retires or I get too old, we're going to fix this place up.'

"I knew what moving meant—all the packing and boxes and trouble, and how worked up you get looking for another place to live. I knew it was one heck of a mess. In Poletown there were people who had lived in the same houses all their lives. Those people just didn't understand what it was like to gather up and move all the stuff you accumulate.

"And it wasn't just the chore of moving that bothered me. My house was special to me. It was where my kids had grown up, and my father had helped us to get the place—it had been such a relief to him to see us settled. He died just the next year, so the house had memories for me. I didn't want to give it up. I could look all over at the work we'd done on it, thinking, 'the boys helped out here, the girls helped here.' One of the last things the boys did was to put up a new roof. We had worked hard for that house. All your life, you're told a home is the best investment you can make. Poor people look forward to it—owning a piece of their own property. It's the American dream; if you own property, you've accomplished something with your life. But along came the city and told us, 'You own nothing. You have no rights.' "

Bernice doesn't remember exactly what she said at that early meeting when, after having sat quietly and listened, she finally stood up and spoke her mind. She was angry. She didn't believe the city's promises of help. She wanted people to understand what was happening to them, what moving would be like. And she wondered why many more people weren't angry and fighting.

Buying up the property, paying relocation benefits, and preparing the site to hand over to General Motors was to cost about $200 million in federal loans and grants, of which the city would have to repay about $100 million. General Motors was going to pay the city $8 million for the site.

To acquire titles to the property, Detroit was using its power of "eminent domain," normally used by governments to condemn and take over private property for a public project like an expressway or public housing. When a government uses eminent domain, it is required to compensate the owner for the condemned property—a process often involving years of court disputes before the government can take title and proceed with its project. But since GM insisted on having the property quickly, Detroit couldn't afford the usual delays. As the Poletown residents were to learn at one of the first community meetings, the city had a powerful new law to rely on. Two months before General Motors announced its plans for the Cadillac plant, the Michigan state legislature had passed a "quick take" condemnation law, which in essence allowed the government to "take" first, and go through any court disputes on compensation later.

The official leaders of the effort to oppose the city's demolition plan (known as the "Central Industrial Park Project" by the city, and more emotionally, "what happened to Poletown" by the people who lived there) were the men who had been involved in planning and raising grant money for revitalizing the Chene Street shopping area. But the most committed and energetic opponents of the city and General Motors were women. Besides Bernice and Carol, there were Carol's mother, Louise Crosby, Ann Giannini, Josephine Jakubowski, and others—except for Carol, most of them middle aged and older, and all of them angry about losing their homes.

If other people weren't as vocal, there were reasons. One was the relocation benefits, required by law since federal funds were being employed for the project. Renters were to receive payments of $4,000 to help cover potentially higher rents elsewhere; homeowners were to be paid "fair market value" prices for their houses, plus up to $15,000 to allow them to buy comparable housing in another area. All the residents were to receive up to $500 in moving expenses, and anyone who moved out quickly was to get a $1,000 bonus. Some residents, particularly the renters, saw the benefits as a windfall that in some cases allowed them to make down payments on their own homes. Some of the elderly homeowners had children who were glad to use the payments their parents were receiving to move their parents, and themselves, into larger houses. The promised benefits didn't buy Bernice's support, however. "They first offered us $11,500 for the house, then came back and offered $13,500. Big deal! We didn't ask to move." There was, she says, no way to compensate people for the memories and the community they were losing. "They took away something valuable from the people, and gave it to GM for practically nothing," she says.

Many more people didn't speak out because they still didn't understand what was happening, or couldn't—or wouldn't—believe it. Others were afraid. Crime escalated in the area immediately after the first article appeared in the newspaper about the city and GM plans. While Bernice was still on vacation, six crimes took place in a small area. In one case, intruders tied up a dog in a plastic bag so that they could break into the home; one of Bernice's sons found it and freed the dog. Bernice and others suspected that the city had a hand in some of the crime, or at least quietly condoned it. "What's better than fear for getting people out of an area—especially older people?" she says.

The city, meanwhile, was pushing its project along with dizzying speed. In mid-July the city council approved the project area, and by the end of the month the city had mobilized title searchers, lawyers, and property appraisers. Door-to-door appraisals began, and in August the city screened and selected members of a "community district council" that was supposed to communicate residents' needs to the city, but was perceived by opponents of the project as representing the city's interests, not the residents'. "They weren't there to fight to save the area," Bernice explains, "but to put us out—and on time."

In the late summer and early fall, residents began receiving green booklets printed by the federal Department of Housing and Urban Development. On the cover was a cartoon-style illustration of two faceless figures moving furniture. The booklet, "Relocation Assistance for Displaced Homeowners," was stamped "For Information Purposes Only," and had a printed slip attached to the outside saying, "The information in this booklet generally describes relocation processes and benefits in programs utilizing federal funds *if and when* such programs are approved by both the federal government and the City of Detroit. At this time no official local, state, or federal approvals have been given to start a project in this area. The City is presently examining the effects that a project would have, not only on the people living in or owning property in the area, but on the economy of the city as a whole." On the inside, the introduction began, "You have just received a 'notice of displacement' from a public agency carrying out a public project with financial help from the Department of Housing and Urban Development. Sometime in the future it will be necessary that you move so that the public project may proceed."

Anyone who had doubted that something serious was happening in Poletown couldn't doubt it any longer. In one case, the booklet set off a tragic chain of events that seemed to symbolize the upheaval in the community. A woman was confused and disturbed by the booklet and went to her priest to ask what it meant. When she got home, she found her purse had been stolen. Totally distraught, she jumped out of an upstairs window; a neighbor who saw the scene suffered a heart attack.

The efforts to oppose the General Motors–city plan intensified. "They didn't anticipate that the Poletown people would organize and fight them," says Bernice. "They probably figured they'd come in, hit us quickly, and have it made—people would panic and leave. Some people did. But not everybody. We turned around and organized, to make sure we got our chance to go to court, and to see if we could beat the system. But we didn't know how strong they were. You always feel that somebody, somewhere, is going to come out and support you. Everybody can't be for this, you think. But we were wrong. They had everyone involved, so they got away with it."

Bernice started writing letters to politicians—her first ever. She hadn't had much respect for politicians before; the response of officials to the Poletown affair made her trust them even less. "I had never really followed politics that much," she says. "I guess I'm just like the average person. I used to not even vote, but then people told me that if I didn't vote, I shouldn't bitch about the people who got elected. So I started to vote, but I always figured there wasn't much of a choice on the ballot. You really don't know anything about these people who become your mayor or your governor. I hadn't really distrusted government before—I just never had had much to do with it directly. I didn't realize that politicians weren't working for people until Poletown happened. Other people had told me about writing to politicians with some recommendation or problem, without ever getting an answer. But I always thought that couldn't be true—that if you wrote a letter, they'd respond. When I started writing letters to politicians about Poletown, I got letters back that explained nothing about what I had asked them and instead completely evaded my questions. So it all came into focus for me; it all came down to, what were they afraid of, what kind of hold did General Motors have, that the company could come in and say, 'If you don't give us this piece of land, we'll build somewhere else'?"

Bernice and her neighbors found it wasn't just the elected officials who wouldn't oppose GM. When they decided to challenge the city's decision to condemn their neighborhood, they had trouble even finding a lawyer to represent them; local and out-of-town lawyers alike balked at working against such formidable opposition. While the leaders of the Poletown Neighborhood Council were pursuing the legal end, then, several residents, including Bernice and other women, tried a different tactic. "Legal angles are alright," Bernice says, "but the legal angles weren't getting us anywhere." Since they weren't getting through to officials or even lawyers, they decided to appeal directly to people, through public demonstrations. "I think if I had it all to do again, I'd start out earlier organizing demonstrations," says Bernice. "There's a message you get across with demonstrations; sometimes it's better than sitting down and explaining things to people and reporters one-on-one; with a whole group protesting, there's a stronger effect on people." One Sunday morning at the end of September, Bernice and several other women picketed in front of St. John the Evangelist Church, close to Bernice's house.

The Roman Catholic archdiocese of Detroit is influential in city politics; previous urban renewal and highway projects had had to be altered to accommodate church buildings. In the case of Poletown, however, the church hierarchy put up no fight to preserve the area's two Catholic churches. One priest bucked the church hierarchy; he was the pastor of the Immaculate Conception Church, in the southeastern section of the proposed GM site, a half-mile away from where the plant was to be built. Fr. Joseph Karasiewicz opposed the demolition plans, and allowed the church basement to be used as a headquarters for the neighborhood opposition efforts. The Immaculate Conception Church was fifty-three years old, and had a predominantly Polish congregation, with some masses still said in Polish. A shrine commemorated the millennium anniversary of the affiliation of Poland with Christianity.

As Poletown residents pointed out, it was the Catholic church in Poland that allowed the Polish people to retain their heritage through years of foreign domination, and the church was currently supporting the workers' Solidarity movement in that country. In Poletown, the Immaculate Conception Church was the only local institutional support for the group opposing the city and GM, and the church and its pastor became symbols for the efforts to save the neighborhood. Some of the most committed activists in the struggle were parish members—older Polish women and men whose community spirit until then had been manifested in parish affairs like potluck dinners. To many of them, the idea of losing their church was as painful as losing their homes.

The other Catholic church in Poletown, St. John's, hadn't shown any signs of fighting for the neighborhood, so it became the scene of the first demonstration. The protest was organized spontaneously; Bernice, Carol, and Ann Giannini and Ann's son gathered at Carol's house, decided to demonstrate, and thought up slogans. Bernice's son borrowed stencils from his art teacher to do lettering on signs. ("After all, it was our first demonstration," Bernice says. "We wanted things to look good.") The women started sounding out their neighbors to see who was willing to join them. Someone thought to call reporters, and an article on the protest appeared in the next day's paper.

Any feeling of small victory was shattered two days later, when HUD approved the first of the federal loans to support the demolition.

Bernice's life was changing. The occasional, once-weekly community meetings were happening more and more frequently, until there was something scheduled each night. The opposition group was exploring every possible lead for support. Bernice was becoming more and more outspoken. Burglaries and arson had increased steadily in the neighborhood, and many people were afraid. "Some people wouldn't come out to demonstrations because they were afraid if their face was on TV, they'd be next in line for arson. A lot of people asked me why I wasn't afraid. I'd be a damned fool to say I wasn't. I was just as scared as the next one. But I had enough anger in me to overcome the fear and go on fighting for what I thought was right. That's what gave me courage.

"It used to be that my way of dealing with trouble was to go into a corner and avoid it. If somebody hurt me, I'd just cry—though I wouldn't let my kids see me cry. But when this happened with Poletown, I just said 'Enough is enough.' I'd had it with sitting in corners not expressing my feelings. Poletown did something to me. They were taking my home away. They were taking things that meant something to me." Bernice used to be "as docile as a lamb," in her husband's words. She wasn't a lamb any more. She had once looked down on demonstrations; now she was out initiating them—even calling them "demos" for short. She had been outspoken within her family before, she says. "But what you do in your house, with your family, is one thing. To speak out in public is another."

Another woman who was learning to speak out was Bernice's friend Ann Giannini. Her family had moved from Pennsylvania when she was two years old, and she was raised on Trombley Street with ten brothers and sisters. Her husband ran a billiard hall in Poletown for twenty-eight years. Ann was seventy years old when the news of GM's plan for her neighborhood broke. "I would say to the newspeople, 'These are supposed to be my golden years, a time for sitting and taking it easy, and here I am out demonstrating instead!'

"I got involved right away when I found out what was happening," she says. "We blasted away at all those officials who came to meetings. They were trying to tell us they'd do this for us, and that for us, and we told them, 'No way. You can't make it up to us.' I stood up and talked. It was the first time I ever did something like that—I was shaky, shaky. But I told them, I said, 'Can you make up for the friends and neighbors we'll lose?' I went to that demonstration at St. John's. We were trying to stir up more opposition, and get people to help us try to save Poletown. I never thought I'd be in a demonstration. Neither did other people—they were hesitant about demonstrating. They'd never done it before either, and didn't want to. We'd talk to them and tell them they had to get out and fight. There was a group of us that stuck together. I stuck with them, because I didn't want anyone to take my house. I didn't want to leave my neighborhood. There wasn't any other neighborhood I thought I'd like to live in. I'd never pictured myself anywhere else.

"I'd say to the officials, 'You find me the same kind of house I have here, where I go two blocks to the grocery store, and where there's a bank right on the corner, and where the kids went to school two blocks away. And a hospital just across the street, and a post office right behind me in the alley.' I said, 'You find me another house like that.' They'd say, 'You know that's impossible, Mrs. Giannini.' And I'd say, 'Now you know why I'm fighting you.'

"So we had our meetings. Just about every day we had meetings, trying to figure out what to do. Women played a more important role than men did. There were more women at those meetings. There were some men, too—like my brother; he had never known any other house than the one we were brought up in and he was still living in. In my house, every time I started going around with the boxes, to pack, I'd start crying. I was mad at everybody. I was mad at my son; I was fighting with my husband. I was saying, 'They don't care! They don't care!' They cared, but they wouldn't show it. The women showed it more. Women are more aggressive, really. I think we find it more natural to go out and fight for what we think is right. I think the men, a lot of the time, just let it go. They figure it's a lost cause. But that's not the attitude to take. Whether it's a lost cause or not, you still have to go to the bitter end.

"People were hurt so badly by what happened to the neighborhood. There was a woman a couple doors down from me, she died from it. She was alone; she had lived peacefully in her three rooms. She wasn't even that old—in her sixties or something. She had a little white cat, and when this happened, I guess someone arranged to have her put in a nursing home, where animals weren't allowed. So the last time I saw her, I was walking up the street and she stopped me. She asked me, 'What am I going to do? They won't let me take my cat. Who's going to take care of it?' I said maybe I could find somebody, or that I'd take it. She was so disturbed that day, but I was in a hurry to get to the store. But next thing I heard, they told me she'd died. She was sitting in her rocker with the cat on her lap and the TV on when she died. It had just broken her.

"I knew all the people here. We grew up together. Ed Niebala, who owned the Chene and Trombley Market, we knew one another. I was up in the store one day, and before I left, he hollered out after me, he said, 'Hey, Mrs. Giannini, don't leave the neighborhood without me. Stick with me to the end.' And I said, 'I'm sticking it out as long as I can.' The next day, we passed through there; my son and I were in the car, and we saw an ambulance. I didn't know what happened. I called my sister-in-law, because she lived on that block, and she said, 'It's Ed. He's gone.' So I went to the funeral and I said to him, 'OK, you told me to stick with you. But I'm not dying yet. I'm fighting.' "

They fought. In October the Poletown Neighborhood Council finally found a local lawyer, Ron Reosti, to represent them and challenge the project in state court. The lawsuit, filed the same day the Detroit city council gave its final approval to the Poletown demolition, argued that the use of eminent domain in this case was unconstitutional, since private property was being taken not for public use, but for the gain of a private corporation. In early December, the judge ruled against them. By the middle of the month, the first Poletown residents were moving out, and the city began demolition work on the Dodge Main plant. City workers also began other work, involving digging holes in front of homes and leaving huge piles of dirt.

The demolition work disrupted any remaining semblance of routine in the neighborhood. "The only job most women had had was taking care of the house," says Bernice. "But nobody wanted to do that any-more. There was sand coming from every direction; you couldn't clean your house if you wanted to. As soon as you cleaned the dust off things, five minutes later there was another layer. The only place you tried to keep clean was the kitchen, so you could cook. Before you could cook, you had to take a rag and wash the goddang dust off. It just seeped through things; even if you closed the doors and win-dows, it would be there. And once they started tearing places down, it was quick. The only thing that stopped them was bad weather, and sometimes they worked in that too."

Bad weather didn't stop the women from demonstrating either. Af-ter the first protest at the church there were others, at city hall and the archdiocese. "When it was time for a demonstration it always seemed to turn cold," Bernice remembers. "It was as if we were being tested—were we going to be strong enough and have enough courage to go out there anyway? It would be raining, or snowing; the weather just worked against us, as if it was trying to get us to just chuck it. But we always went. We froze our tootsies off sometimes, but we went out. We knew that what we were fighting for was worth it."

Pat Barszenski, a young registered nurse who lived in Poletown and was involved in the opposition efforts, later conducted research for a master's degree thesis on the effects of forced relocation. She has the-ories about the women's role in fighting the city and General Motors. "The women went through all the stages everyone else went through—the same shock, and denial, and depression. But they were astute; they never lost sight of the fact that their rights were being violated. Other people wanted time to think about what was happen-ing; they wanted to assimilate facts. But these women understood im-mediately. They were the first to recognize the injustice. They might not have known at first whether General Motors or the city or both were to blame. But they knew simply that what was happening stunk. There was conflict for them too, of course. On one hand, there was the personal loss of their homes and community, but they were still able to cope and fight for what was right. They were angry, and they channeled that anger in a constructive way.

"As time went on, you saw an evolution in these women. At first, their anger led them to simply blurt things out at meetings—things that could be dismissed by people who wanted to. But then they changed; as they became more vocal, they were more articulate and sophisticated. They would let the officials hang themselves on their own words. The women put themselves out front. They were the conscience of what was going on."

There were more impromptu demonstrations. Bernice and the others also spent long hours working in the Immaculate Conception basement—by this time support had come from Ralph Nader in Washington, who sent in a few community organizers to help with the opposition effort. Residents were working on mailings to appeal to groups and individuals for support, and were talking to reporters, trying to get them to see and report on the human side of what was happening, not just the official version of "reindustrialization" and new job predictions.

For that matter, inconsistencies in job predictions were already surfacing. In applications for federal loans and grants back in the summer of 1980, the city had boasted that the project would create tens of thousands of jobs, including jobs for two shifts of workers at the Cadillac plant, demolition and construction jobs, and spin-off employment in the surrounding area. That prediction was then chiseled down to six thousand jobs in the plant, and not necessarily new jobs, but jobs simply being retained, since two existing factories were closing. The six thousand figure was eventually pared to three thousand, and Bernice and other residents were skeptical about even that estimate, since there was talk about the new factory using assembly-line robots. The City of Detroit, which constantly pointed to jobs and the economy as the reason it was destroying a neighborhood, never did get a commitment from General Motors to actually provide a specific number of jobs. In addition, none of the jobs predictions took into account the jobs lost when Poletown businesses were evicted. Some of the almost 150 small businesses eventually opened shop elsewhere, but most of them went under, including a coal company near Bernice's house that had employed close to one hundred people.

The city, meanwhile, continued to bulldoze its project through, both literally and figuratively. In January, a mass condemnation hearing was held; residents were searched as they entered the hall where it took place, and the hearing consisted, according to Bernice, of the city reciting the list of parcels of property it wanted and the judge granting them, automatically ruling against any objections.

Things weren't going any better in the courts. The Michigan Supreme Court agreed to hear an appeal of the lawsuit in which residents argued that the use of eminent domain in Poletown was unconstitutional, and in late February the court ordered that the demolition work stop until it ruled on the case. But in March the court ruled five to two against the residents. The majority opinion parroted the city's line: "The power of eminent domain is to be used in this instance primarily to accomplish the essential public purposes of alleviating unemployment and revitalizing the economic base of the community. The benefit to a private interest is merely incidental." In a dissenting opinion released later, however, one judge worried that the case could be used as a precedent in similar situations elsewhere. "With this case," he wrote, "the court has subordinated a constitutional right to private corporate interest. As demolition of existing structures on the future plant site goes forward, the best that can be hoped for, jurisprudentially, is that the precedental value of this case will be lost in the accumulating rubble."

Having lost in the state courts, the residents challenged the city in federal court, arguing primarily that the project violated federal environmental law, since, in a required study of the environmental impact of the plant, the city had failed to consider reasonable design alternatives. In fact, in the GM plans for its new factory, of the 465 affected acres, 174 were destined to become parking and landscaping. Poletown covered 176 acres. A Washington, D.C. architect came up with a plan for the site that showed how, if GM were to consolidate buildings and construct a multistory parking structure instead of a sprawling parking lot, the plant could still be built and Poletown saved. The residents had argued from the beginning that they weren't opposed to building the plant; it was common in Detroit for factories and residential areas to coexist in close proximity. It was the unnecessary destruction of Poletown they objected to. The court didn't see it that way, however; in April the federal judge ruled that the city had given sufficient consideration to alternative designs. General Motors had rejected the idea of a multistory parking lot on the grounds that it would increase traffic congestion and air pollution.

The court setbacks were disillusioning. "Still, we had to go through the process," Bernice says. "We had to try everything we could. It was our right to use the courts, and at the beginning we had a lot of hope. We sat in there and watched, and for the first couple of days, it seemed the judges might be for the people. But then you could see the change, as they seemed to be more attentive to the other side. And then you realized that you meant nothing to them. And the governor was like the rest of them. When we were in Lansing for the Supreme Court case, several of us visited him in his office. He sat there and told us to our faces that, well, he didn't know all the facts, but he'd look at the options—but that we did need jobs in Michigan, and after all there were six thousand jobs at stake here. So there was the governor, admitting he didn't know all the facts, but agreeing with General Motors without knowing them. How can you trust politicians like that—who sign papers agreeing to a project, without knowing all the sides?"

As the demolition of homes began in April 1981, the large, plain letters spelling out "GENERAL MOTORS" on top of the corporate headquarters downtown became more visible from Poletown. That month, the city once more demonstrated its deference to the corporation when GM applied for a 50 percent, twelve-year tax abatement on the new plant. During hearings, several city council members expressed misgivings about granting GM the tax break when the city budget was already running a deficit. But GM responded with heavy lobbying, including threats that without the tax break it would consider building elsewhere. The council gave in, and voted eight to one to grant the tax break—worth about $72 million to the corporation over twelve years in city, county, and school property taxes.

By that spring and summer, Poletown looked more like a war zone than a neighborhood. As more residents left their homes, especially when the courts ruled against them, looting and arson began in earnest. Looters were after anything of value at all—aluminum siding, stained glass windows, solid oak doors. Fires broke out all over the neighborhood; at one point, fourteen fires raged in one twenty-four-hour period. One of them leveled the elementary school building near Bernice's—a school that until then had been attended by Albanian, Yugoslavian, Arab, Polish, American Indian, black, and white children. The fire blazed most of the night; Bernice and Harry watched from their house, concerned that it might spread.

Still more people left the neighborhood, and their homes were torn down. What kept the others going when their cause was obviously hopeless, Bernice says, was the even stronger feeling of community that continued among the remaining residents. A sense of humor also helped. When the demolition work made it hard for cars to get around the neighborhood, Bernice, Harry, and Carol started using bicycles to ride around on the torn-up roads to watch for strangers who might be arsonists or looters, and to talk with other residents who remained. Neighbors dubbed them the "Poletown Patrol." When a water main broke on Mitchell Street, turning the street into a muddy stream, Bernice and her neighbors put up a sign renaming their block "Mitchell Creek." "We were learning to survive," Bernice says. "We couldn't have without humor. It helped us to put what was happening out of our minds for just a while."

The fight for their homes apparently lost, the remaining residents concentrated increasingly on simply saving the Immaculate Conception Church, as a symbol of the community. In February, the archdiocese had agreed to sell the church, reportedly for over one million dollars. Bernice and others demonstrated in front of the downtown archdiocese headquarters, carrying signs saying "Sold for thirty pieces of silver." What followed over the next months was an emotional fight, with the archdiocese demanding that the priest leave his parish, and residents becoming more adamant about wanting the church saved. At one point, General Motors tried to save face by offering to move the church building somewhere else, but the archdiocese declined. The cardinal of Detroit was retiring in May, however, and Poletown residents pinned hopes on the new archbishop, who was Polish. But he refused to reconsider.

In the middle of June 1981, residents began a last protest—an illegal occupation of the church basement that went on even as workers began to remove some of the statues and relics in the church, and after all utilities had been turned off. "We'd sit in the basement in the dark, singing our songs," says Bernice. "We had a theme song, 'Holding Out in Poletown'; we'd sit there on the floor and sing. Father Karasiewicz would come around to check on us; he couldn't come in, but we'd go out and we'd sing it with him."

On July 14, Detroit police arrested the occupiers. By coincidence, Bernice wasn't in the church when the police surprised the residents and began making arrests of people who wouldn't leave. The demolition of the church began the next evening, and went on all night and into the following day. On July 16, as the church was being leveled, several residents took out their anger in a demonstration in front of the General Motors headquarters, where they took turns demolishing an old General Motors Oldsmobile.

Bernice and her husband were among the last residents to move out of Poletown. It was to take another few months before they found another house; in September 1981 they moved away from the rubble and muddy empty lots that had been their community.

They moved to another section of east Detroit not too far from where Poletown had stood. The factory, which was to be completed by May 1983, underwent several construction delays. Ann Giannini moved to a house about ten minutes from Bernice by car, and together they were determined to keep people from forgetting what had happened to their community. They started doing little, symbolic things: Residents put up a cross on the GM construction lot where the church had been; Ann and Bernice wrote to GM asking that one of the roads on the site be named for Poletown and another for Father Karasiewicz, who died six months after he was transferred from Immaculate Conception and his church was torn down. They also went to automobile shows where General Motors was displaying its newest line of cars, and distributed "Poletown lives" stickers.

When Cadillacs finally came off the assembly line in the new plant, Bernice got a certain pleasure from learning that the cars had some problems that required recalls. "I don't sympathize one bit," she says. "I always said if you go around destroying homes and churches the way they did, you'll get yours—not by the hands of the people, maybe, but by the hands of something bigger than us." The plant still isn't operating to full production capacity, and Bernice believes it never will. Years after Poletown was razed, she still gets calls occasionally from people whose homes are threatened by corporate expansion plans; she goes to talk to them, to share her experiences at Poletown.

There's a fire department not far from Bernice's new home, and when they first moved, she kept waking up at night. "I'd hear those sirens, the dog would start howling, and I'd jump out of bed, thinking I was still in Poletown and another fire had started. Now I've accepted that I'm not there anymore. But little things bring back the memories. A big problem is not wanting to fix up this place; I keep it clean, but don't go out of my way. It's not home—with that 'quick take' law it's hard to call anything home anymore the way we used to. Everything in the old house, Harry and I did ourselves. The city and GM took it away from us. We fought—you have to fight, for the principle of the thing, and to let other people know it can happen to them if they're not careful.

"The thing is, no place is safe anymore. You drive around, and wherever you go, you see more buildings being torn down, more 'urban renewal.' It's not for the little people, either—not condominiums that sell for $90,000. The little people are the ones who get pushed out. It's like it was with the Indians, the way when white people found minerals on their land, they made the Indians move.

"I'm not safe even in this house. It's close to the airport; if they decide to expand that in our direction, I could lose this place. I've learned things, though. Poletown was a new experience for us; we learned what's going on outside our homes, outside of raising our families. I think we lost because we had lost sight of what corporations and politicians were doing. I was too busy surviving with my family, trying to protect my children. But while I was busy with that, I didn't know that the very thing I was working for and protecting, my house and my community, were being threatened. They've taken an important part of my life away from me, but I learned I can fight back. And I will again, if I have to."

"We've Found the Enemy"

Gale Cincotta

3

"We said, 'We've found the enemy, and it's not us.' Until then, all the organizing had played one group against another. White people were told the problem was blacks. Blacks were told the problem was whites. And Hispanics were pitted against both. Our object was to take all that anger and energy, and channel it constructively."

*I*n the mid-1960s, Austin, a working-class community on Chicago's far west side, was a "changing" neighborhood with a litany of problems. Racial tensions were high, for instance, and many realtors took advantage of the tensions to make a quick profit. These "panic peddlers" created fast turnover in real estate (landing a commission every time housing changed hands) by going door-to-door telling white homeowners that black families were moving into the neighborhood, and that they should sell their homes quickly before property values plummeted. Police protection and other city services in the neighborhood slackened, and when absentee landlords allowed housing to deteriorate, city inspectors were often lax in enforcing housing codes. Schools were overcrowded, while funding, textbooks, and teachers went to wealthier districts. Bank capital was also being drained out into the suburbs, as banks and insurance companies "redlined" inner-city neighborhoods like Austin—literally drawing red lines on maps to mark the areas they considered to be bad risks, making it impossible for people within those areas to get loans or insurance policies.

Gale Cincotta lived in Austin at the time, and as she saw it she was faced with a choice: either move out or become an activist. She chose to stay. "People tend to think that if you can't get a bank loan, there's something wrong with you; or if your kids aren't learning, there's something wrong with the kids," she says. "It's important to know it isn't you, or your kids—instead, there's something wrong with the system that has to be changed. When I first realized that, I got angry. And I've stayed angry. The only alternative is to move—but what's the difference if you move? If you don't have the same problems there, you'll have other problems. So I think you have to come to a point where you stop and dig in and do something about the problems around you. When you look around your neighborhood, you start to see what's happening—people at school boards making decisions affecting your kids' education, realtors and banks controlling the community. Instead, *you* have to control your community."

Just to hear her talk and watch her in action is to know that Gale isn't intimidated by other people's power. She is self-confident and outspoken; people call her a "tough cookie," and mean it as a compliment. In her mid-fifties, she's heavily built, which she accentuates by wearing bright flowered dresses. She has blonde, curly hair and wears large-framed glasses. She talks, laughs, and smokes nonstop. She's energetic, and uses her energy—apparently with real self-satisfaction—to oppose the extremely powerful interests that she sees as unfairly controlling people's lives and communities.

In the twenty-some years that Gale has been a community activist, the powers she's battled have included, among others, the local school board, landlords and realtors, banks and insurance companies, multinational oil companies and politicians who cater to them, and the military establishment. Not forces to be taken on lightly. And not forces that an ordinary woman challenges on a daily basis—unless, as Gale says it was for her, it's a matter of survival.

Gale was born and raised on Chicago's west side. She married young and had six sons. When the first son was old enough to start kindergarten, Gale and her husband, an automobile mechanic, bought an Austin "two-flat"—a house with a separate kitchen upstairs and enough room to accommodate their extended family, including Gale's parents, grandparents, and an uncle. When the neighborhood began to change and other white families started moving out, Gale didn't want to leave. "I think I'm like most people—I don't like to move," she says. "Especially in our neighborhood, where we had everything we needed, then what was the point? Austin had a park, a couple of swimming pools, even a nine-hole golf course. There's every denomination of church imaginable, housing from brick to frame—some of the homes in the central area are old frames with little ballrooms on the top floor! And to get downtown you just get on the el or the express bus and zip down. So why would you want to move? But I learned that if I stayed, I had better get involved, because otherwise, for starters, my kids wouldn't learn anything."

Gale's first fight, with her children's education such an immediate concern, was for better schools. The resources Gale employed were drawn from the main experience she had had up to that point—managing a family. "A lot of what's called 'research' is really just common sense," she says. "If you have to run a household on very little money, you learn things. I don't have a college education, but I've figured out a budget, I've paid a mortgage, I pay my bills regularly. When you deal with these things, they make sense to you. And then

you can start making the connections. You look at the board of education. They have just so much money; if they put all that money in one
area, they don't have it to put in another. Well, I knew if I did that
with my children—if I said, 'I like you better, I'll give everything to
you,' that would obviously be unfair. But that's essentially what the
board of education was doing with all our kids."

She discovered proof of that discrimination by going to the board
of education and attending hearings and poring through school board
records. What she found was solid evidence that in her neighborhood, in addition to overcrowding of schools, there was underfund-
ing: About $250 was spent on each pupil in Austin, compared to some
$700 per pupil on the wealthier far north section of Chicago. And the
funding discrepancies appeared to be deliberate; school board bound-
aries were being changed to accomodate wealthier areas to guarantee
them adequate funds.

Gale then tried to have the inequities remedied. She had attended
neighborhood block club meetings before, and had listened to the
way people talked about their problems at those meetings. Inevitably,
she says, someone would blame the neighborhood's problems on the
black people who were moving into it. Gale says she always questioned that assessment. After conducting her own investigations and
concluding that the school problems were the fault of the school
board rather than the newcomers, she took the information to the
school principal and local aldermen. These officials ("people I
thought were supposed to take care of things for me") refused to
recognize the problem, and dismissed Gale as a troublemaker.

"What you figure out then is that the principal is worried about his
job and his record in running the school, and would rather have you
be quiet so that he can look good. These people don't want to make
waves; they've got their own mortgage to pay off and a couple kids in
college to support, and they want that promotion. So you realize that
people in their position are afraid to take responsibility. Either you're
going to take the responsibility yourself and maybe end up very un-
popular, or you have to move. I still didn't want to be pushed out of
the city into the suburbs; I didn't want to send my kids to private
school either."

So Gale got together more and more of her neighbors who had
children in the school, and started to advocate change through the
Parent-Teacher Association. "PTAs just don't do that much traditionally," she says. "They're seen by the schools as a way to make cos-
metic changes, like help make sure there are curtains in all the
rooms—rather than as a way to push into the really important issues."

But the PTA had a structure and certain rules that Gale could use to her advantage, including regular meetings where issues could be raised, and access to school records and the board of education. When Gale and her friends heard about school board hearings, they would put out advance bulletins announcing when and where the meetings were taking place and what subjects they would cover. If something especially important came up, they called the press to be sure the story got out.

And gradually their active presence brought about some improvements. New audiovisual equipment was shipped in, more textbooks were provided, and an addition was built onto the elementary school. All along, though, Gale found that she and her friends had to watch officials carefully. The parents had fought for a new middle school, for instance, to relieve overcrowding in the other schools. They not only proposed the school, but also suggested ways to build it quickly using prefabricated walls and construction workers on two shifts. But even after their idea was approved there was a delay, when the parents discovered that builders were planning to raze a hundred homes for the school site. Gale and the others got officials to postpone construction for six months, and eventually to agree to build the school on ten acres of vacant land a few blocks away. "Some planner had just said, 'Here is the middle; this is where the school is going,' " Gale says. "Well, we said, 'Look, it's a school for sixth through eighth grade; those kids can walk a few blocks!' "

The school fight taught Gale a number of valuable lessons—including to be on the lookout for such shortsightedness on the part of officials. It also taught her one of the most important qualities of an organizer: patience. "With that middle school, from the time we first started fighting for it to the time the doors opened, it was five years," she says. "My son never went to that school; by the time it was finished he was too old. But you learn to interpret little things as victories, to keep you going. The first meeting with officials, where they agreed to consider the proposal, was a victory. Then there was this good decision, and that one. So the whole five years, we were celebrating each step."

While they were fighting for better schools, Gale and her friends also learned to look around and determine what was causing other neighborhood problems. That led to more confrontations—sometimes very lively ones.

A new community organization was forming in Gale's neighborhood. The Organization for a Better Austin (OBA) was started by followers of Saul Alinsky, a community organizer whose theories and books on communities' self-determination are the bible for most community organizers today. Alinsky worked in Chicago, and Alinsky-style groups sprang up all over the city in the mid-sixties. When OBA was getting started in Austin, Gale attended meetings skeptically at first, afraid that they would be a repeat of earlier unsuccessful block club attempts, some of which had failed because of racism. Gale had some differences of opinion with OBA at first. "They had their strategies, and I had mine," she says, "only I wasn't calling them strategies at the time." But Gale was a natural for community organizing, and ended up becoming very active with the new group, eventually serving as its president for several years.

In her PTA days, Gale had already begun to recognize a pattern to the decline in her neighborhood. When she and other school activists had the attention of the press at school board meetings, they would point out the other problems that concerned them—real estate abuses and declining police protection among them. OBA helped Gale to take that work further. "What we were told back then was that changing neighborhoods were a natural phenomenon. But we started to see that there was a lot of money being made in changing neighborhoods, and that they were being racially changed on purpose—*targeted* for change. First the realtors would come in, start on a block or two, and pass out leaflets, telling white people they had better get out or they would lose money. Then the banks wouldn't give mortgages and the insurance companies wouldn't write policies. Then police would be assigned somewhere else. In the meantime, people would deposit their money in the banks in these 'changing' neighborhoods, but instead of investing the money back in the neighborhood, the banks put it into suburban track development. There were ads in the papers telling you that you were practically un-American if you didn't move out there to the suburbs. There wasn't any money for loans if you wanted to buy here in the city, or rehab here, but for a low down payment and good terms, you could move somewhere else. *That's* no natural phenomenon! Through the community organizing, people were able to identify who the enemies really were. They weren't the people moving in or out; they were the realtors, the banks, and the savings and loan companies."

In true Alinsky-group fashion, OBA dealt with its "enemies" in a very direct way. In 1969, for instance, by looking at ads in the papers and at "for sale" signs in the area, the organization was able to conduct a study showing that, although normally there would be about thirty-five realty companies doing business in Austin, there were about *three hundred* companies at the time. The companies, OBA found, had developed effective tactics. "They put up 'for sale' or 'sold' signs all over, so that it looked like the whole neighborhood was up for sale," says Gale. "They also printed flyers with pictures of black people, with the caption, 'Meet your new neighbor.' Or they circulated listings of property for sale, including everything within a couple of blocks around you, so that it would look like you were the only one who wasn't selling and moving out.

"And were they making money! You can figure that they turned over a block in maybe six months. They made a commission on every house in the block, plus maybe a commission on houses where the new people coming in had lived. Plus, somebody made a commission on the houses where all these people were moving. And the realtors scared people so badly that they would sell really low. Some of the companies bought up the property themselves, and then turned it over for huge profits."

OBA responded by going directly to the offices of the realtors to demand that they either behave professionally or leave the neighborhood. OBA asked them to sign nonsolicitation agreements, and picketed the offices of firms that refused. They also filed complaints with the Chicago Commission on Human Relations and with the Department of Registration and Education, which licenses realtors. And they tackled other housing problems as well. When city inspectors ignored housing code violations by slum landlords, OBA members set up their own housing courts, usually in church basements, and would call in the building owners themselves to try to get them to comply voluntarily with housing standards. To back their allegations, they collected evidence: The ad hoc housing court charges were punctuated with photographs of substandard conditions, jars full of cockroaches, and dead rats. If the landlords refused to come to "court," OBA activists weren't stymied; they would pile into buses—dozens of the members, mostly women, black and white, with preschool children in tow—and picket the landlords' downtown realty offices. On one occasion they took a dead rat with them, and plunked it down on the landlord's desk for emphasis.

In an extreme case, they would go into the landlord's own affluent neighborhood and start talking to neighbors, or drop off leaflets at all the houses on the block featuring pictures of the landlord and of problems in the buildings. Once, OBA learned that a particularly recalcitrant landlord they had been working on was the coach of a little league team. They went to one of the team's games—attended by the parents of the players—and picketed and handed out leaflets that asked, "Did you know that Coach is a slumlord?" The "Coach" acceded quickly to OBA's demands and started correcting the problems in his buildings.

Confrontations like that were obviously exciting; as one woman who was active along with Gale puts it, "When you got a large number of people together that way, feeling their oats, it could be exhilarating. There were fun times. It's always enjoyable to win." Ironically, the actions not only embarrassed the individual landlords into improving conditions, but also inspired city housing inspectors to do their jobs better, since they realized that when they made accusations against a landlord, OBA would back them up with plenty of evidence, and if necessary, pressure from plenty of people.

By this time Gale was spending more and more of her days on OBA work. Meetings were often held three or four times a week, and even before Gale became the organization's president, she was in charge of several issue areas, including education, real estate, and urban renewal. "It was a very busy time, very hectic," says a friend of Gale's who lived in Austin and was also involved with OBA. "I know Gale was intensely busy; a lot of us were, and Gale did more than the rest of us. She was pivotal to the organization. She was very practical; she didn't sit around wringing her hands; she could identify problems easily and had a good sense of what would work and what wouldn't. She was really interested in winning, and had the energy—and made the time—to do what was necessary to win. She had many family responsibilities, lots of kids to take care of, and her parents and grandparents all living in the same house. But I think her sense of responsibility simply went beyond her home; she's like a traditional woman who branched out. She's very conservative, very ethnic, in certain ways. She doesn't drive a car. Even when she became a paid staff person, she still didn't get a checking account. She would just take her paycheck to the bank, buy money orders to cover her bills, and deposit the rest into savings. She had never ridden in an airplane until she got involved in community work, and was terrified of it at first."

What motivated her, Gale says, was her anger. "When you look carefully at what's going on around you, you have to get angry," says Gale. "I got mad, and that gave me courage. I was never intimidated by people—the school board, for example. All I could see was that these people were making decisions affecting my kids' lives. I guess I must have thought enough of myself from the beginning to fight back, and not worry about what people thought of me. Maybe that comes from having a solid family, and my own strength, and a lot of friends.

If you do this kind of work, you can't be fretting about who likes you. You've got to have your own base of support—be it your family or a network of friends. Or when all else fails, you have to at least be able to say to yourself, well, I've got this big dog who likes me, and is glad to see me come home so I can feed him!"

Family has always been important to Gale. Her father immigrated from Greece, and when Gale was growing up, her parents worked hard in the restaurant they owned. Gale spent much of her childhood surrounded by adults. "Raised in a family with older people, as an only child, you probably get to do a lot of things other kids don't get to do," she says. "In our house or in the restaurant we always had lots of people over, talking. The kids weren't chased out; if you wanted to sit at the table you could. And the talking went on and on. You had lunch or dinner, and three hours later you were still at the table taking about politics or what have you. At our friends' houses it was the same way. I was never told that women don't participate in those discussions. My mouth was going the whole time, and I got questions answered. I think, too, that living with older people you learn a lot— just seeing what happens to them. My grandparents lived to their nineties, and I learned what their problems and concerns were.

"When I started doing this work, I found it doesn't really have to take away from other things. You can still have your family life and your friends. Some things have to give, of course. When I got busy, I taught my boys how to cook, how to sew, how to run the washing machine, and how to like Kentucky Fried Chicken! My youngest grew up going to organizing meetings. My husband might have liked me to stay home with the kids all the time, but he and the kids adjusted. The children learned to take care of one another. And my husband was always the steady one; he was like a clock—home the same time every day and on weekends. I made sure that birthdays were always celebrated, and holidays. I was always home then.

"And some things do change. When you get active like this, your outlook is different. You've started to control your life. Sure, it's hard work; it means long hours. But it's different from other kinds of work. It's like the entrepreneurs in this country, the small business people. My mother and father worked sixteen hours a day, but because it was their own business they didn't mind. With community organizing it's the same. It's different from working for a corporation, where you can always get fired, and where the end result is just a product—whatever it is they decide to make and sell."

After working with the Organization for a Better Austin for a while, Gale began to recognize the limitations of the Alinsky organizing style.

For one thing, although the memberships of the organizations were made up to large extent by women, the staff organizers and elected leadership were almost exclusively men. Gale was the first woman to be elected president of any Alinsky-style organization in the country, and men in the organization placed bets against the chances of her winning. "Up until then," she says, "it was always the women who did the work, and the men who got elected. And even when I ran, although I was obviously qualified, people in the organization made a point of saying, 'Do you want a man or a woman for president?'—not who was smart, who could do the job, or whatever."

Gale infused a different kind of life into the organizing, says one woman who worked with OBA and has continued to work with Gale. "She had a different style from many of the men organizers at the time. She wasn't caught up in the mystique that many of the men were caught up in. For them, organizing was almost a romantic thing. For her it wasn't; it was a practical need, and she was more straightforward than someone trying to spin a yarn and attract you to a big idea. It was good for me to be able to deal with a woman—a strong woman involved in the decision making the way she was. That's always a blessing when you're around only men."

"When I first got into organizing," says another woman, "there were certainly a lot more male than female staff, and then here was this very, very strong woman who was at the head of her organization. What I found was that most of the people who got involved in community organizations *were* women. Maybe that was because they had the responsibility of taking care of the home and children, and they carried those concerns about their home and family a step further, into the community, and got more involved than their male counterparts. But the thing was that a lot of the community organizations' staff were men. And I think it was important that Gale encouraged women to get into leadership roles, because I feel that men and women think about certain issues in different ways."

"Gale has encouraged more women to get involved," says another organizer, a man who has worked with her for several years. "Her own involvement has definitely had ripple effects, and has contributed to the growth of other groups around the country. Women were often active in these groups, but not as leaders. Today, much of the leadership of community groups is women, and Gale has done a lot to encourage that just by her example. She's also influenced many women going into community organizing as a career."

Gale brought other changes to organizing at the time as well. Another problem she had found with the Alinsky-style organizations was their focus on turf. Each group had a clearly defined geographical area that it represented, and it worked only on the problems in that particular area. This sectarian approach seemed inefficient to Gale. "Obviously you can't have an impact on everything right here, in x number of blocks. To win some of our issues, we had to be able to go out and get citywide support. We had to go to people—church people, for instance, and say how we thought it was immoral that our kids' schools were so crowded, or that there were such serious housing problems. Knowing how much we needed other people, it just didn't make sense to say that the world began and ended in our little neighborhood."

So, together with OBA organizers, Gale began to reach out to other groups—first simply by talking to them, inviting them to OBA actions, and having meetings with them. They then tried to form a citywide coalition, which failed, as Gale sees it, because initially the groups were working on such different concerns. But the attempt did open the door for communication among the groups; they each learned what the other was working on and with what tactics. "That coalition effort, which we thought at the time was such a bust, really started to break down the traditional barriers between groups—the barriers of 'I'll do it myself, my way,' " says Gale. Eventually two of the groups, OBA and the Northwest Community Organization, began cooperating more formally. An organizer was hired to cover the neighborhood between the two groups, and the "Our Lady of Angels Real Estate Committee" was formed, funded largely by area churches. That created a solid block of neighboring organizations, which in 1970 banded together into a coalition.

The problems in her Austin neighborhood, Gale was gradually realizing, were not limited to Austin, or even to Chicago, but were shared by urban communities all over the country. The causes of the problems were equally broad: Federal housing policy was affecting neighborhoods as much as city agencies were. Although federal laws were passed in the late 1960s to make it easier for people of low and moderate incomes to own their own homes, for instance, federal regulations tended to protect the banks and other lending institutions rather than the home buyers. Some of the regulations actually encouraged fast foreclosures on mortgages. And some homes sold under federal housing programs were substandard. So Gale went from picketing slumlords to challenging federal agencies like the Department of Housing and Urban Development, the Federal Housing Administration, and the Federal Home Loan Bank Board, which regulates savings and loan associations.

In the meantime, OBA had become a popular training center for organizers from around the country. After spending a summer there, these organizers would go back to their communities and form similar groups. Gale encouraged formation of these groups and maintained ties with them, and in 1972 she helped bring them together for a national conference on housing.

It was the first conference ever to unite neighborhood groups from around the country working on housing problems, and it was successful beyond even the organizers' hopes. Over two thousand people from thirty-eight states converged in a church hall in Chicago—so many people that the conference proceedings had to be broadcast on video monitors in the hall's basement, which held the overflow. An impressive roster of politicians attended, as well as reporters from such newspapers as the *Boston Globe,* the *Baltimore Sun,* the *Cleveland Plain Dealer,* and the *Kansas City Star,* and from the magazines *Newsweek* and the German weekly *Der Spiegel.* As one organizer puts it, "The outside world probably realized better than we did what was happening. We just saw the conference as another step in fighting on the issues. But the outside world saw it as 'something new was happening.' "

That "something new" was a new kind of unity. According to Gale, "At that conference we said, 'We've found the enemy, and it's not us.' Until then, all the organizing had played one group against another. White people were told the problem was blacks. Blacks were told the problem was whites. And Hispanics were pitted against both. Our object was to take all that anger and energy, and channel it constructively."

It was agreed at the conference that a national organization should be formed to work on neighborhood concerns. A month later a founding committee made up of delegates from two hundred local groups that had attended the conference met in Baltimore. Out of that meeting, National People's Action was formed, and Gale was the natural choice for chairperson. The name for the organization is appropriate: The organization is national, uniting neighborhood groups to allow them to work on nationwide problems. It is also very definitely about "people," ordinary people like Gale: whites, blacks, and Hispanics from working-class, mostly urban communities. And it is certainly about "action." The night NPA was formed, delegates attending the founding meeting learned that the Secretary of the federal Department of Housing and Urban Development was guest speaker at a dinner at the Washington, D.C. Hilton, so they boarded buses and traveled from Baltimore for an impromptu "meeting" with him to raise their concerns about housing problems.

Since that night, Gale can often be found in similar scenes, characteristically at the head of a crowd, with a microphone in her hand, gesturing as she talks in her strong, enthusiastic voice to the crowd or to the official she is confronting. If she isn't leading a crowd, she is as likely to be running a planning session with representatives from some of the approximately three hundred local groups that have ties with NPA. Or, she can be speaking before a cheering audience of thousands at an NPA annual convention, engaged in negotiating in a small meeting with a federal official or a banking or an insurance company executive, or testifying before Congress.

Although the group started by working on housing issues, it quickly moved into other areas. When energy prices suddenly went up in the 1970s, for instance, NPA made energy policy a chief concern. The group also discovered that banks weren't the only institutions to redline; insurance companies did too, and NPA began confronting them. Gale laughs about the time an insurance company attempted a wholesale cancellation of about ten thousand policies in a "risky" neighborhood—Gale's. "I just thought to myself, 'Oh, boy. You people *are* stupid. Go ahead. *Try* and cancel my policy!' " The cancellations were stopped.

The organization has also made health care costs the subject of conferences and workshops. And in the 1980s when the military budget skyrocketed while social services were cut back, Gale started criticizing exorbitant military spending. "The very best 'defense' policy this country could have would be strengthening its neighborhoods," she argues.

Among the staff at NPA, members of local groups active in the organization, and her friends, Gale is known for her passion about issues and for her leadership qualities. "Gale's leadership has always been significant," says an NPA staff person. "Gale makes the difference. She has an incredible ability with people, and an important sensitivity to what people are saying, what they need. She can sit in a room with twenty different people from twenty different groups and have a sense of what might bring them together. She has good instincts about people and what motivates them. Often when you're doing this kind of work, you have to second-guess what the 'enemy' will do next, and I think all organizers acquire instincts—but Gale's are usually the best.

All this isn't magic, of course; it's just a quality that some people have. I don't know where people learn it—in kindergarten, at home, or in block club meetings. But Gale has it."

Another staff organizer says, "One important thing that Gale brings to this work is that, to the people we work with, she's one of them, rather than someone who has a college background, and has done all these glorious things and then comes back to talk to people about what they should do. She's really one of the folks. She helps keep staff honest about what people are really interested in. When we come up with ideas, she'll say, 'Will our people really give a damn about that?' Sometimes as staff we forget about the effect of things on folks we work with. Gale doesn't forget."

"Gale acts as a spokesperson," says a friend who has watched her work. "But a good thing about Gale is the way she develops leadership in other people, too. She recognizes others' contributions, and always acknowledges them. So she'll be the spokesperson, yes, but she might bring in two or three other people, to help do negotiating with officials, or just to tell what has happened to them specifically. She encourages people—both by being what she is, and by allowing them to make full use of what they are. She's not pedantic at all. When she's dealing with people, it's never with the kind of attitude of 'I know something that I'll impart to you.' She just encourages them to say what they know. Then she reinforces it, fills in around what they say, and sums things up."

Gale is also credited with an unusual ability to "make connections"—to understand the broad cause of a local problem and assign blame to the appropriate powerful institution or institutions, while understanding the interconnectedness of the institutions themselves. She says she learned this through experience. "I learn through reading some—but mostly through doing. I still ask a lot of questions, just like when I was a kid. In Washington, when people say something I don't understand, I ask, 'What do those letters mean? What do you mean by that?' People talk in shorthand; we all do that sometimes. We have to learn what all the numbers and letters of regulations mean. But you do learn; it's *just* shorthand, not something that's beyond you. You learn how corporations function, who regulates—or is supposed to regulate—whom. You're learning all the time, which is fun. You learn without even knowing it.

"The way my mind works, it all fits together. There are other people who take things and separate them out to understand them. To me that's difficult. Some of the people I work with tell me I talk like James Joyce writes, in a stream of consciousness, weaving back and forth from one issue to another and how they're related. But that's the kind of thinking that's missing in Washington. The Department of Energy doesn't talk to Housing, so they build homes that aren't insulated, don't have solar panels, and lose energy through big windows. It just isn't coordinated. If that's because they're jealous of their turf, I say they're sick. It's as if something hangs over their heads and pollutes their minds. So it's up to us to go in there and say, 'Look, if you do this, it's going to do this to housing,' or 'If you do this, it'll do this to energy use.' "

Gale and her organization do "go in there" to call attention to problems. Their tactics are the same as OBA's were, and often the NPA confrontations with government and industry representatives are reminiscent of OBA's dealings with realtors and slumlords. The only difference is that the problems being addressed are broader, and therefore the opponents can be all the more formidable. But it seems that none is too formidable for Gale. Among the targets of NPA actions have been the Department of Housing and Urban Development, the Department of Justice, the Department of Energy, the Federal Reserve Board, the Business Roundtable and the National Association of Manufacturers, the American Council of Life Insurance, the American Bankers Association, and the American Petroleum Institute.

An American Petroleum Institute convention in Chicago, for instance, once coincided with an annual NPA convention. Because NPA was concerned with the effect of higher energy costs on low-and middle-income families, they decided to "crash" an industry-sponsored cocktail party. "We asked around for whoever had a suit or a dress," Gale remembers. "We gathered about seventy-five people together that way, went to the top of the Hancock Building, and walked in on Exxon International. We freaked them out. We didn't really think about it until later, after we'd left peacefully, but God, they're all so guilty, they probably thought we were terrorists, out to kidnap them or something. Suddenly there we were in the middle of them—not looking at all like them, because they were all white men, and we had women, and blacks, and men with beards! I think it's important for our people to see how these executives live. But it's just as important for them to see us, and to know that there's no place to hide—not even the top of the Hancock Building, where they think they're so high above the people. They didn't even have a security cop, they were so sure of themselves. Next time they'll have one— probably more than one. And that creates jobs." She laughs. "Jobs you learn to take where you can get them!"

An oil company executive was the target of a similar NPA action in Ohio. The action was part of a "Reclaim America" campaign in several cities one week that fall, which, Gale explains, was designed to show graphically who the controlling interests are in the country. In Cleveland, NPA planned to pay a visit to the president of Standard Oil of Ohio. "They were ready for us at his house," Gale says. "And they were ready for us downtown. So we went to this hunting club where we knew he had a membership. It was classic—there were eight buses full of people, going through the woods over rolling hills. Four buses went in one way, the others went the other way, and then you came on this idyllic scene that looked like a movie shot through gauze!"

The SOhio executive turned out not to be there, but the NPA people weren't disappointed. "It was lunchtime, and all these people were eating, looking like Barbie dolls with their riding habits and little blond pony tails and little caps and riding crops. And in came our people, singing our theme song, 'When NPA comes marching in.' "

Singing and music typically embellish NPA actions. In October 1980, a "Reclaim America" event was held in Chicago, which inspired the larger campaign two years later. In Chicago, the sixty-piece Paul Robeson High School marching band participated, along with about fifteen hundred members of NPA affiliates, in an event that involved a plane trailing an NPA banner overhead and a rented cruise boat in the harbor near the Chicago loop.

The cruise boat was dubbed the Santa Maria II. It was Columbus Day, and the American Bankers Association was holding a convention. NPA had tried in vain to get several of its leaders into the convention and NPA onto the convention agenda, to address the bankers about ABA lobbying to repeal two important federal antiredlining laws. When the ABA refused the organization's terms, NPA decided to stage a rally to make a point about bankers' power. The scheme was to play on the idea of "reclaiming" America—landing the boat and planting an American flag on the shore of Lake Michigan. The theme was broader than just redlining. "The banks are on oil companies' boards," says Gale. "They have huge lines of credit to the energy companies. In fact, you can tie every issue back to the banks."

Forty busloads of NPA members, including the marching band, converged from different directions on McCormick Place, where the ABA convention was being held and the NPA boat was to land. Aboard the Santa Maria II were Gale and other leaders from NPA affiliate groups. The buses and the boat communicated by walkie-talkies. But when it came time for the boat to land, Chicago police blocked the docking area, and the Santa Maria II had to turn back to dock where it had started out. By this time, the band had struck up "The Star Spangled Banner," "This Land Is Your Land, This Land Is My Land," and other patriotic songs and NPA theme songs. Cheers went up from the crowd when the airplane appeared overhead, trailing the message, "National People's Action Reclaims America!" Gale and the others from the boat raced across town to where the crowd was waiting. One police officer was heard to say, "These people put on a class demonstration!"

The efforts sometimes pay off. NPA has an impressive list of gains: Among others, it lobbied successfully for federal antiredlining laws and a law requiring the Department of Housing and Urban Development to reimburse individuals who were sold substandard housing under federal programs. NPA has also negotiated—with Gale doing the actual wrangling—with insurance companies and banks for hundreds of millions of dollars in grants and low-interest loans for local reinvestment programs, including several pilot low-income housing construction and rehabilitation projects around the country. In Chicago alone, large banks have agreed to make over $200 million available in low-interest loans for housing projects in previously redlined communities. Gale's tools in getting the banks to agree to the loan programs were the federal antiredlining laws she had lobbied for.

Other accomplishments are less easily quantifiable. "I think the most important thing to me is seeing the changes in people, just seeing them develop and feel good about themselves," says Gale. "I go to a lot of annual meetings around the country, and I see these changes all the time. I've seen them in friends of mine, in women I met when we were first involved in school issues. There are five of us who are especially close; we were from different backgrounds, but back then we were all home with our children. Now we're all involved in organizations and careers. We've talked about it, and we agree that our experience back then made a difference in how we feel about ourselves. Just having to run meetings, or put together events, or deal with bigger issues made us see that we could really do something. And this happens to people all over the country. That's exciting to me. Even if it's just one time, at one meeting, that a person speaks up, *that* has to affect her personally, I think. If she was never there before, and never comes back, the fact that it has happened still has to affect her. She begins to understand what makes things happen to her—that there's nothing wrong with her."

Gale herself has changed. She isn't afraid of flying anymore. And she has gained confidence. A woman who has worked with her for several years tells about an early community meeting where Gale spoke once, years ago: "It was a Saturday meeting at a little church on the west side," the woman recalls. "I wanted to see Gale in action, so I

offered to give her a ride. I was sitting with her before she was supposed to speak. I looked down and saw that her hands were shaking.
Today, she takes on anybody, and is comfortable speaking anywhere."

Gale still lives in the two-flat in Austin, in an area that is now almost
entirely black. Driving west, people who live there say, you can tell
when you get to Austin, because other areas that weren't organized
have turned into slums. In Austin, there are still some abandoned
buildings, but there's also the feeling that people have more control
over their lives and neighborhood. Two of Gale's sons still live at
home, and her parents live upstairs; Gale cooks many of their meals
for them. Doing her community work, Gale says, took "adjusting."
When her husband died several years ago, Gale's youngest son was
fifteen and she wondered what effect all her traveling would have on
him. But the family managed. "Whatever I do, I'm *me* in my home—
not somebody important who's just visiting. I'm still my kids' mother,
my parents' daughter. My family is important to me. It's also a good
leveling thing for people involved in work like this; you've got all
this 'important' stuff going on in your head, and someone says, 'Ma,
I don't have clean socks,' or 'What's for supper?' It helps balance
your life.

"When I'm not working, I like to go out to movies. I don't like
pictures that talk about problems; I don't like to be depressed. I love
walking into a movie house and within five minutes forgetting everything else. I also keep up with friends; we go out to dinner, go to each
other's houses, go out for birthdays. I used to do some oil painting,
but don't have time for that anymore. For a hobby, I enter contests—I
love to fill out the forms. I don't know why; maybe it's the discipline,
just having to sit still for a few minutes. My girlfriend says, 'What do
you get out of it?' and I just say, 'Well, at least I can remember who I
am, and my address and zip code!' I like a lot of the traveling I do—
not all of it. I enjoy going to different cities and seeing the differences
and the similarities. You have to get used to traveling alone. Things
can be so hectic; sometimes you enjoy being alone, having dinner in
your room, watching television. And I like to read, especially on
airplanes—magazines, and the latest mystery."

Gale has never forgotten what made her first get involved in community work. "I remember those school board meetings," she says. "I
think there were more hysterical people there than at any other meetings I've been to. That's because people may think that, even if they
didn't quite 'make it' in their own lives, they were going to see to it
that their *kids* would. But then they found out the kids weren't going
to either, so there were heated meetings, with very angry people. It

was women, especially, who came to those meetings. I think community organizing is a natural for women; it's right there in the neighborhood. You can take the kids, or figure out the babysitting among you. And it's a place where women can show what they can do.

"The whole process is very slow. I get impatient," she says. "I tend to think things should have happened two days ago, or last year. But especially when you're dealing with large issues—like energy policy, interest rates, and military spending—you have to interpret your gains gradually.

"There are always the skeptics, of course. With any issues we took on, there were people who said it isn't going to work. They thought we'd never get all those groups together in one room for the first housing conference, but we did. Then when we took on the Federal Housing Administration, people said, 'It's too big for you; it's a federal bureaucracy.' But we figured it out, step by step. And with our legislation, people had said, 'The banks are too big.' But we beat the bank lobby. People are always saying you can't do it. But maybe you can. You can do a piece of it. At least you can build a base for someone else to build on. If you say you can't do it, you won't even touch it, and then of course you can't do it. Doing this work is just a matter of self-confidence, and having people behind you. People call me a leader, but I say, well, if you don't have people behind you, you're not leading anything. What we have is people power. Other people have money power, or 'political' power. We've got to fight with our people power."

Gale obviously loves what she does. "I'm stubborn; maybe I'm naive, but I operate on the idea that things are going to happen, that if you work hard enough and get enough people behind you, you're going to win." And "winning," according to Gale, is getting to a point "where people really have a say in their lives, where *they* call the shots."

"Education's the Thing"

Maria Fava and Mildred Tudy

"The more you learn—about local politics, about community issues—the more you want to learn. You become thirsty for learning. Education's the thing that makes people most comfortable with themselves, self-confident—even the most quiet person, the most passive person."

*F*acing west from Brooklyn, New York, there's a perfect view of the skyline of Manhattan—some of the world's highest-priced real estate and headquarters for some of the world's most powerful corporations. A short subway ride away and worlds apart from this affluence and power is the north Brooklyn community of Williamsburg, among the poorest neighborhoods in the city. Poor and working-class families, over a third of them headed by single women, live there and in the neighboring community of Greenpoint, in simple homes, tenement buildings, and public housing projects. The community has a mixed population, with black, Hispanic, Jewish, Irish, Polish, and Italian residents. Over the years it's had its share of problems, including racial tensions, crime, declining industry, and high unemployment. But the residents also have an enduring sense of community, exemplified by an unusual women's organization that is based there, the National Congress of Neighborhood Women.

Maria Fava has lived on the same block since she moved to Greenpoint in 1955. A Mexican American born and raised in Laredo, Texas, Maria married an Italian man stationed in Texas with the air force, and moved back with him to his Italian neighborhood in Brooklyn, relinquishing her own cultural identity in the process. A few years before Maria settled in Greenpoint, the federal government had built a housing project not far from the Italian stronghold there, and the community had been up in arms. In 1953 Mildred Tudy's family was among the many black families to move into the Cooper Park project; Mildred has lived in the same two-bedroom apartment there ever since, and has become a tireless community activist in the process.

Today Maria is a counselor on the staff of the National Congress of Neighborhood Women; Mildred serves on its local advisory board. Their separate stories tell how women in Williamsburg and Greenpoint are fighting for their community while successfully bridging gaps between races, and between low-income women and feminism.

A ring that Maria wears says a lot about her, and about her surprising brand of feminism. It's a "mother's ring," and Maria proudly points out the significance of the four birthstones set in it—"This one's for Johnny," she says. "He was born in July. This one's Anthony, October. Penny, February. And Joe, March." Maria bought the ring for herself, when her husband left her after thirteen years of marriage. His leaving marked a turning point in her life. "I found strength I didn't realize I had. I had to *make* this strength, for myself and for my family." Until she happened on NCNW in 1975, though, Maria didn't think of herself as a feminist or an activist. "My personality is quiet," she says. "I usually don't like to fight—I always think you can accomplish more with sugar than with vinegar. But when I have to fight for my children, I do. And I guess I've always been a feminist in my own way; I've always fought for what I think is important. To me that's what it means to be a feminist—being able to fight for your rights, your community, your children, and other women."

Growing up, Maria had longed to leave Laredo. Her mother worked hard to support the family, and Maria dropped out of school in the ninth grade to go to work in a five-and-ten store. "My mother was an obedient wife," she says. "She married my father, and knew she'd stay married for better or worse. I didn't want that kind of life for myself. I always wanted to marry someone who'd take me away to a big city, and care for me so I'd never have to work. And when we married and moved here, my husband was a good man and a good provider. He wasn't perfect, but he loved me and I loved him."

Part of loving him meant adopting his culture as her own. In that neighborhood, Italians usually married other Italians, and Maria's mother-in-law had a hard time accepting her at first. "I was the only outsider; I had to fight to leave my culture behind, not because I wanted to, but because I wanted to belong here. It was hard—everything was different: the climate, the culture, being in a city. I learned Italian from my mother-in-law, and learned how to cook Italian food. I'd never learned to cook Mexican food. God knows, growing up I had been tired of eating beans, but here I found myself craving them. I didn't even know how to make tacos or flour tortillas—I'd try and they'd come out terrible. But I learned how to make manicotti from scratch! I wanted to please my husband and my in-laws." Her children never learned Spanish.

Maria's first baby was stillborn, and she went to work as a salesclerk for a short time at Gimbel's department store in Manhattan. She quit her job when her other children were born, to concentrate on raising her family. Her youngest son was a year old when her husband left her. "I was a survivor; I tried to fight to keep him, but he found another woman who could help him with his debts. I faced a big decision then, whether to go back to my mother and start all over again, or stay here alone with the children.

"I had my pride; I didn't want to go back. So I stayed, and we went on welfare. It was the first time in my life that I was on welfare. We had been very poor back home, but my mother worked; we all worked. Here I had to go on welfare for the children, but made up my mind that I would better myself, and get a job." She threw herself into her new goal, going to school at night to study for her high school equivalency exam, volunteering at her sons' school, going to community meetings—all with the purpose of "bettering" herself. "You learn to carry on," she says. She failed the equivalency exam the first time she took it, but didn't give up, and the second time she passed. Going to college was never part of her plan, but in 1975 Maria's life changed when she walked into the office of the National Congress of Neighborhood Women.

NCNW was a brand-new organization then. The idea for setting up an organization for low-income women had originated in 1974, with a meeting in Washington attended by women like Barbara Mikulski, a grassroots activist in Baltimore who was then a city councilwoman and later became a U.S. representative and then senator, and Jan Peterson, a community organizer and director of an antipoverty program center in Williamsburg/Greenpoint. "We felt there needed to be a woman's voice that poor and working-class women could relate to," says Jan Peterson. "The way the women's movement was going, it wasn't designed and structured for low-income women, and didn't have as priorities the kinds of issues that poor women would be interested in. It was clear to us that for the women's movement to have a vehicle for organizing poor and working class women, it needed to be neighborhood based, and focused on issues of family, community, and race and ethnicity. There were certain things that women said at that meeting in Washington that would still be true today. One thing was that they didn't want to be called 'poor women' or 'low-income women' or 'welfare women.' They didn't want to be described by their income; instead, 'neighborhood women' came up pretty early on as the term that people felt comfortable with. They also didn't want a big national structure with a national office in one place, and everyone else 'out there.' They wanted a small national structure that was more of a facilitating organization, based in a community and active in that community."

The resulting organization opened its doors in Williamsburg/ Greenpoint in 1975, with Jan Peterson as the board chair and later its executive director. The group's first project was an ambitious one, a neighborhood-based program to offer women associate of arts degrees. "It was obvious that education and control of education were vital in this whole issue of empowering neighborhood women," she says. But she knew from her own experience that it had to be done properly. She came from a working-class family in a small town in the Midwest, and was the first one in her family to go to college. "I saw firsthand how my family wanted me to go to college so that I'd have a chance to 'make it,' but they really had all this ambivalence, and anxiety that they'd lose me in the process. When I'd come home they'd say, 'Now you think you're smarter than us; you're not one of us.' There's something wrong with the university system, the way it is set up to make people become part of something new, apart from where they came from. You can see it in this community. People feel that you can be ruined by getting a degree. And often people *are*—not because of learning, but because they're forced to choose a new set of values or they don't make it. We found that the people who were the *least* helpful in working with poor, working-class women were their educated sons and daughters, because if they went to school and came back, they often felt either superior or resentful. When you're forced to give up part of yourself, you resent the group that reminds you of what you've given up."

The challenge, then, was to provide women with an educational opportunity without forcing them to leave their community or choose between two sets of values. The solution was a program co-sponsored with a community college, to provide courses taught in the community and relevant to community issues, as well as to provide course credit for community work. Many colleges were experimenting then with adult education and off-campus programs, but the co-sponsorship structure that NCNW set up was unique, and became a model for several other communities around the country. It wasn't necessarily easy: "We didn't know what we were doing at first," says Jan Peterson. "We had to learn everything from scratch—how to deal with university departments and politics, how to balance theory and practice if you really want the neighborhood to *be* the university." She had worked with a coalition of community groups and had obtained a large pool of Comprehensive Employment Training Administration (CETA) funds for the groups; she was able to take a small portion of

those funds to recruit and hire twenty-five women from the neighborhood to work in agencies and service organizations. Most of the
women were immediately enrolled in the college program.

Maria was one of them. She was interested in a job, not college, but
when she went into the organization's office for an interview she
found that it was a package deal. "I had never dreamt of going to
college. I decided to do it for the job, and just figured I'd quit the
college program later. And every time I had to write a paper, I wanted
to quit. But once I started, I realized there was so much for me to
learn. Education became so important to me; my priority became to
set an example for my children. I'd tell them they couldn't drop out of
school, but instead to look at what I was doing. It was hard; I had to
stay up very late to do my homework after the children were in bed.
But the more you learn—about local politics, about community
issues—the more you want to learn. You become *thirsty* for learning. Education's the thing that makes people most comfortable with
themselves, self-confident—even the most quiet person, the most
passive person."

While she attended classes, she was also working, at a legal services
office in south Brooklyn, and at a battered women's shelter set up by
NCNW. She gained valuable on-the-job experience in tenant advocacy,
counseling, and legal interviewing. At the women's shelter she worked
on the telephone hotline, and was able to help women with information she was learning at legal services. She also continued to be involved in community issues that had an immediate impact on her life
and her family. A local police precinct had been closed, for instance,
so Maria and other women in her neighborhood would attend meetings at the next precinct to petition for adequate patrolling of their
blocks. On her own Maria also started a support group in her home
for single mothers. Support was a key concept for NCNW; the women
who were enrolled in the college program had a "buddy system" to
give each other personal support when they needed it—to help out
when children were sick and they couldn't attend classes, or to give
encouragement when they were tired and ready to pack it all in. The
method worked; the first group of women, including Maria, received
their associate of arts degrees at the end of 1977.

Maria was still on partial welfare; she diligently reported everything
she earned, every raise she received. "The only reason I wouldn't let
go of welfare was because of the children. I wanted it for the Medicaid
coverage. So I know how hard it is on welfare, how it encourages you
to lie—I had the same fears and insecurity as anyone else." In 1979 she
starting working for NCNW full time and went off welfare completely.

She was already changing, from a submissive wife to a more self-confident, assertive woman. She was in the office one day and happened to answer the phone when someone called from a college in Manhattan to say that they had scholarships that they could offer if there were local women who were interested in receiving training toward a certificate in counseling. "I'm the quiet and passive type, right?" Maria says. "But maybe not *so* passive—I just said right away, '*I'm* interested!' and gave my name and made an appointment to go in." The certification program lasted a year; when NCNW received grant money to do outreach to single mothers, Maria was hired as a counselor.

NCNW was maturing, too. On a national level it was tied in with grassroots women across the country who were developing and running innovative programs to help low-income women to become self-sufficient. On a local level, it had developed an advisory board made up of women leaders from various organizations throughout the community, and brought these women together regularly in issue task forces to advocate for improvements in such areas as housing, day care, health, education, and employment training. Meanwhile, the organization was coming up with practical methods to develop and support women's leadership. "We figured that if groups like Weight Watchers and Alcoholics Anonymous and other support groups were such a powerful mechanism, why not develop support groups for people who are OK—women who were trying to hold their lives and communities together?" says Jan Peterson.

The organization was also learning the basics of how to work together in spite of racial and ethnic differences. Whenever meetings or conferences were held, time was set aside for dealing with issues of race and ethnicity. "We didn't want to get into the 'who's worse off' stuff—but we didn't want to avoid hard issues, either," Peterson says. "So from the beginning we absolved each other from guilt, realizing that nobody knows well how to deal with people from other groups. We allowed time for teaching each other how to do it more effectively—so that, for instance, one group might explain that they didn't want to be called 'Spanish-speaking' women, but 'Hispanic women,' without implying that the other group was dumb or prejudiced not to know that already. We talked about what each group expected other groups to know about them; we forced people to put their requirements on the table, not just wait for someone else to make a mistake. And when we sat together in rooms and talked across the racial and ethnic lines, we found connections. For all these women, children reign supreme. Each group had a different view at first of who was more family focused—but when they started to really talk to one another, they heard that every one of them had strong feelings about their families, particularly their children."

Education emerged as a focus of the organization, which gradually developed a systematic community-based educational program. In addition to the college program, NCNW now offers high school equivalency classes in both English and Spanish, English as a second language, adult basic education, and skills training in such things as bookkeeping and word processing. The organization provides day care and day care referrals, and when it became clear that women involved in the educational programs were as concerned about their teenage children as about younger children, NCNW initiated an alternative high school program for teenage drop-outs—complete with a cooperative child care center for the teens' children. The organization continues to offer counseling and support at all levels; Maria is head of the counseling program.

"Counseling women means basically encouraging them to go on," she says. "My own strength comes from all the problems I encountered—I feel that I've learned from them. There were plenty of times when I wanted to give up. My persistence kept me going—that, and the support I got, and the way I felt when I finally accomplished something. It's important to share that—to share the fears and how I overcame them. Sometimes I feel like it's obvious, or it's repetitious, but I'm surprised—that particular woman may not have heard these things before, and it encourages her."

"We've learned something important about empowering neighborhood women," says Jan Peterson. "When we initially pushed to have day care centers established in communities across the country, for instance, in our zeal to get going, we didn't take time to think about who the heck was already *doing* the day care in the community—the mothers, the aunts, all the women who were wonderful at taking care of children. Most of those women weren't even consulted in the planning and development of the day care centers; instead, we used people with professional degrees. There's a quality that's lost in that kind of professional orientation. That doesn't mean you don't want professionals in there—the ideal is a partnership of professionals and grassroots women. In our infant child care center, two of the women interns running it are on welfare, and another woman is in our college program. It's the most wonderful, warm place; it's like being in a family kitchen; you see these rough teen fathers coming up and holding and cuddling these little babies, or being mothered themselves by the staff people there. I keep telling other women, if they feel depressed about what's happening in the world, they should spend an afternoon in that room—they'll come away feeling hope about what we can do.

"Having someone like Maria doing counseling is the same sort of thing. She's from the community and committed to the community— and she feels that because she had a chance, she wants to make sure that other women get it. She can be tough when she has to; she's not just sitting there holding people's hands. I don't know how many hundreds and hundreds of clients she's worked with; she's done this counseling over and over again. And obviously she can reach them in a way that nobody else—with a Ph.D. or a masters in social work—is going to be able to."

In 1981 Maria got a chance to buy the house she was living in; her son encouraged her and her children pitched in, and she bought the home. And when the NCNW college program was expanded to include a bachelor of arts degree, Maria enrolled. "I've always felt that God has taken care of me," she says. "I don't think I'd be the same person today if my husband had stayed. I'm a better person; I've made a life for myself. I used to worry about growing old alone, without my husband, without my children. I'm fifty-five years old now; everybody's gone, and I find I *like* it! I've learned a lot, I have a lot to give— and I wouldn't want to go back to the way I was."

From the point Mildred Tudy moved into the Cooper Park housing project in Greenpoint, she ended up raising her children alone much of the time, too.

Mildred was born in 1927 and lived in Macon, Georgia until she was three, when her parents moved to East Harlem. Her mother was well educated, having finished high school and a year of college. She had four daughters after Mildred, and at the age of twenty-four she suffered a recurrence of the typhoid fever she had had as a child, and died. Mildred's youngest sister caught the disease from her mother and died six months later. "During the mourning period, my father said to me, 'Now *we* have to raise these children.' " Mildred was six years old.

Her father never complained about not having a son. "He just said he would train us to do everything that he would teach a boy; he taught us construction work, how to paint; whatever he could do he taught us to do. It stuck with some of us longer than others. I like to know the fundamentals of things, to make things by hand, and I was always asking questions. He tried to answer my questions as far as he could; then when he couldn't, and I still wanted a more definite answer, he'd look at me and say, 'Listen, I am the father, you are the child—you have to take my word for it. Now, no more questions.' That worked; I ended up using the same thing on my kids.

"Dad had only a fifth grade education, but he saw the benefits of education in my mother. When she was dying, he promised her that whatever happened, we were going to stay together and get educated." Another promise was that the children would be raised as Catholics; Mildred's mother had spent months in a Catholic hospital and was impressed with the nuns there. Mildred went to Catholic school until the third grade, but when her younger sisters entered school it became too expensive, and the children were put into public schools. "The public schools were better then than they are now," Mildred says. "Children were treated the same—whether they were black or white. The teachers were mostly Irish, and what teachers! I'll never forget Mrs. O'Connor, in the fifth grade. She taught us poetry—drilled it into us really. But she did it with such animation and such joy that we ate it up. And that's what teaching should be like."

If young schoolchildren were all treated equally, by the time they reached high school the equality broke down; black children were generally directed into vocational schools, and white children into academic high schools. Mildred longed for the academic route, and applied to the Julia Richman public high school for girls on the east side of Manhattan—but heard nothing in response. Her grandmother was an active member of Adam Clayton Powell's church in Harlem; Powell was an alderman at the time, and he used his influence to get Mildred into the school. Only a tiny fraction of the girls in the school were black; Mildred worked her way onto the honor roll and was elected student government secretary. The night she had to give her acceptance speech, she was overcome with nervousness. "My sister was a sophomore then and she was sitting in the balcony. I just stood there, a little, skinny, puny girl, and couldn't get started—now you can't stop me, but then I couldn't get started. My sister was more outgoing than I was, and she just yelled out, 'Mildred, go on! We're behind you!' And all my buddies up in the gallery shouted, 'Yeah, we're behind you!' So I made my little speech."

Back then, New York City high school students were routinely given civil service exams and placed in government jobs when they graduated. Mildred put off her employment and attended Fordham University for a year before taking her job with the immigration bureau on Ellis Island. She decided that she could finish college later;

World War II was imminent, and with everyone else in school, the family needed money. She loved her work, which involved direct contact with immigrants applying for their working papers and citizenship. "I'd watch them get sworn in, see their tears of joy. This was the country of hope, symbolized by the Statue of Liberty. Today, I get so angry sometimes because our country doesn't live up to that image. But in those days I wasn't angry—I was bland. I had my job. I hadn't been troubled yet by any racism. And any obstacle that had come up, we'd been able to overcome it."

When the war ended, Mildred got married; ten months later she gave birth to twins. ("I didn't even *want* children," she says. "I thought my mothering days were behind me! But my experience with my sisters helped me in coping with my instant family.") She and her husband moved north of Manhattan to the Bronx; he was a building superintendent and started working in automechanics, so Mildred helped with the building maintenance work, keeping the coal burner going, and working the garbage dumbwaiter. But when she became pregnant again several years later, she realized they needed more room, and she applied for an apartment in public housing. "Public housing seemed like such a step up—the places were designed so well, and were new and clean. We got accepted into a new federal housing project in Brooklyn, in Greenpoint—I didn't even know where Greenpoint *was,* and I worried about being so far away from the rest of my family. But I was grateful to get it, so we moved anyway."

It wasn't until after they settled in that Mildred learned how controversial the housing project was in the community. "The European immigrants had come over in the 1860s and 1870s, and felt that this was their bailiwick," she says. "Where the housing went up it had been a wasteland—with a few secondhand shops and some goats that the Italians raised for cheese. But they still thought it was their community. The federal government built that project—the city would never have done it, because of the politics. But for those seven hundred families moving in, it was wonderful."

By this time Mildred's marriage was not going well. Mildred's husband had come up against racism during the war, and had returned determined to escape poverty and prejudice. He set up a successful auto body shop in the Bronx, and stayed there much of the time, while Mildred raised the children in Greenpoint. In 1956 she became pregnant with her last child, but the marital problems continued. In 1968, they split up for good, and her husband moved to California.

Meanwhile, Mildred became an activist. After the federal government had built Cooper Park, it was up to the city government to provide such basic services as paving the sidewalks around the housing. The families were surrounded by mud for years. "They had put up these beautiful buildings—we had a laundry, even a nursery," says Mildred. "But there was such disdain for this project that the city didn't pave it. I guess they kept hoping we'd go away." Instead, they organized a tenants' association. Mildred and several others called a meeting to get it off the ground; they got a book on parliamentary procedure and learned how to run meetings and elect officials. Mildred was elected secretary. The Housing Authority sent them letters warning that they were acting in a "communist fashion," but that didn't deter them from organizing; by then doctors were telling them that they weren't going to make house calls anymore because their cars kept getting stuck in the mud.

At first the group got promises, but no action. Then in early 1961, they went to the office of the Brooklyn borough president, who was a Democrat, and threatened that if they didn't get their pavement, they would start registering every one of the families in the project as Republicans. By April the sidewalks were paved. "I turned into a 'joiner,' " Mildred says. "It made sense—I had learned about the power of organizing from my grandmother; her church was always getting things done. She had had me out picketing for jobs with the rest of them when I was seven. So now I was doing it for the betterment of my family—and plus I *liked* it; I got a charge out of all the involvement!"

Mildred became president of the PTA, taking on teachers who weren't doing their jobs. "There were some wonderful teachers, like the ones I'd had. And then there were others, some of them racist, and acting out their racism on black boys mostly. I told one of them, 'My son is getting to hate coming to school, and getting to hate you. I don't want him to be that way—I want him to have a wonderful experience with learning. So woman to woman, I'm asking you to shape up and be fair.' She told me later that she learned something from that; she had two sons herself."

Mildred also became active in her own church. *Finding* a church wasn't an easy matter, though. Since childhood she had gone back and forth between the Catholic church and her grandmother's Baptist church. "As you get older you realize there's just one God, and that all these different churches and doctrines are really just different ways to worship that God. I felt more like a Baptist than a Catholic. But when I moved, I had promised that I'd make novenas to the Blessed Mother to thank the Lord for getting us that apartment. So I started taking the children to the Catholic church, only we found that when we sat down in a pew, people would move away from us. We knew we weren't welcome there. I continued going for a while just to make the novenas, but it was bothering the kids, so I just started my own Sunday school at home." Eventually a local Italian Baptist church started actively recruiting among the blacks in the housing projects; so many Italians had moved out of the neighborhood when the projects went up that the church desperately needed new members. Mildred's children started going first; she joined in the early 1960s.

The racial tensions in the community had continued, and in 1961 the situation worsened when an Italian youth was stabbed by a black youth in a fight in a laundromat. "All the vengeance from the years of people not wanting that project, and having it imposed on them—it all came out then. They threatened to blow up the projects, to get rid of us all. There was terrible tension. We're located in such a way that you have to go through the white section to get to the subway or the buses; there's no way to walk around it. Black boys and men had trash cans thrown at them; I had to send my son across town to live with my stepsister so that he could get to school without being hurt. Finally the Commission on Human Rights came in—like they should have nine years earlier—and started holding meetings in the community on intergroup relations. They got churches involved; there were some excellent leaders, and meetings every night of the week for a while. And slowly, some of the organizations started working together; we learned more about them, and they found out that we had expertise that they could use. Gradually we realized that the politicians had been fooling us *all*. Not one new building had gone up in that area since the projects were built—every time the community had asked for something, the city said there weren't any funds. City officials knew we were divided, so they didn't do anything for us. We learned a lot on both sides."

It was the kind of lesson in cooperation that NCNW would build on successfully years later. The existing church and civic organizations started working together on little crusades: In a campaign to get a traffic light installed at a dangerous intersection, for instance, women went out with baby carriages and blocked traffic to call attention to the problem. Then there were other issues to tackle, such as holding sit-ins to get a school principal removed who had been violating board of education standards, and demanding that a new school be built.

As Mildred came into contact with a variety of groups, her own involvement broadened. "They say busy people just get busier," she says. "Once you're involved in one thing in the community, you learn about the other issues and organizations. And things spread. When women start getting involved in different things, you have better communication; you figure out that what's effective on one issue might work on something else." She joined the hospital advisory board, and fought to keep up services and retain good doctors on staff. When there was new construction in the community, blacks and Hispanics united to insist on getting some of the jobs; Mildred joined a weeks-long demonstration in which women stood in front of bulldozers to stop construction work until their demands for jobs for minorities and women were met. The civil rights movement was in full swing; in 1963, Mildred took her daughter to the massive civil rights march on Washington.

"We were all fired up by Martin Luther King, Jr.," she says. "We came back from that march knowing that we wanted our own organization. There were the Italian organizations and Polish organizations, and we had our tenants' group and the PTA, but we had no organization that you could identify as a black group. We wanted something for perpetuating our culture, even for *learning* about our culture." So a group got together and contacted a black professor, who helped them assemble materials and start a weekly black studies project. The program caught on, and developed into the Crispus Attucks Center, named after the black Revolutionary War hero. The center sponsored cultural programs and classes, and was then funded to provide summer remedial education for youth. Mildred was employed by a community action program at the time, but in 1969 when the Crispus Attucks Center received year-round funding, she was asked to become its director. Under her direction, and with federal funds, the center expanded to offer high school equivalency classes, adult basic education, job training, and job placement, in addition to the ongoing programs in black culture.

In the 1970s, Mildred went back to college for her own degree—commuting an hour and a half to attend classes in the evenings and on weekends. She graduated in 1976. Federal budget cuts under the Reagan administration hit the Crispus Attucks Center hard; it had to move from its own address into a Lutheran church basement, and went from twelve staff people to two—Mildred and one other. The organization still provides after-school tutoring, and adult basic education one night a week. And it's still a center for promoting black culture. ("We refuse to go out of business!" says Mildred.) She is happily remarried, to a man she met through her community activism. "We're both very spiritual people; we don't do anything without God. You can't, and succeed. It's a very deep, satisfying feeling to be able to accomplish things for yourself and your community—and for me God has been the moving force. And it was my father who taught me what was possible—he always said there was nothing a man could do that we couldn't do, and that our mother could do *everything*."

By the time NCNW got under way, Mildred and Jan Peterson had met and shared ideas; as a leader in the community, Mildred was recruited to join the organization's local advisory board. "The key to a successful urban community is having groups relate to one another," says Mildred. "We need to cooperate to raise the standard of living for everyone. We need to share experiences and expertise. This sort of thing has to be worked at, and most of the time it's the women in the community who are doing the work. And it's an enriching experience for everyone. In this community we've brought forces together, and we're all better for it."

Environment
and
Public Safety

"The Tongue of Angels"

Mary Sinclair

5

"To keep going—to keep remembering that it was ideas I was fighting, not people—I had to internalize passages in the scriptures, like the passage by Saint Paul, 'You can speak with the tongue of angels, but if you have not charity, it's like clanging cymbals.' "

*I*n early 1983, Midland, Michigan, the small city where the Dow Chemical Company is based, received national attention when dioxin, a deadly chemical manufactured by Dow, was found to have leaked into the nearby Tittabawassee River. The local newspaper, the *Midland Daily News,* ran an editorial praising the "people who have gone out on limbs to ask questions about chemicals and their health effects in the Midland area." The same editorial went on to pay tribute to an earlier maverick:

> Mary Sinclair was the prototype in Midland of the lay citizen challenging the conclusions of the establishment. Mrs. Sinclair stood up to ostracism and criticism with a great deal of courage. Now many Midlanders are realizing that some of the objections she raised about the Midland nuclear plant had merit. Perhaps even more important, she brought about public discussion that otherwise would not have occurred.
>
> This latest brush with scientific/social/political controversy ought to lead the community to further consideration of the role of the "troublemakers" in its midst. They are an essential part of the ongoing process of democratic government, and Midland owes them a debt of gratitude.

To Mary, the belated praise was ironic. Thirteen years earlier, after publishing several letters to the editor from Mary raising concerns about a proposed nuclear power plant, the *Midland Daily News* had written her to say in effect that that was it—if she wanted any more of her views published, she should pay for an ad.

Mary's involvement with the issue of nuclear power had begun, simply enough, as scientific interest. It was during the 1950s. Congress had decided to encourage commercial application of the technology that had been used in bombing Hiroshima and Nagasaki, and had established the federal Atomic Energy Commission, charged with two arguably conflicting duties: promoting nuclear power and protecting the public from its dangers. The AEC's record as a regulator has since been severely criticized (as is that of its successor, the Nuclear Regulatory Commission), but it performed its other function with zeal. Through aggressive promotion the public was led to believe that nuclear power would be a miracle of sorts—safe, clean, and cheap. Among experts there were serious doubts about the technology, but the general public was oblivious to them.

Mary wasn't. At the time, she was working for the Library of Congress in Washington, D.C., helping to put her husband through law school. Part of her job involved handling then-classified AEC documents on nuclear energy research, which acquainted her with the emerging technology. Over the years she continued to follow the nuclear industry's progress—and problems—in the scientific literature she read regularly. At first she was all for nuclear power. "I knew of the problems, but thought they existed because the technology was so new," she says. "We'd solved other technological problems, and I was confident we'd solve these. I had faith in technology, and was optimistic about nuclear power working out."

By 1967, though, the problems still hadn't been solved, and Mary knew it. That year the local utility company announced plans to build a nuclear power plant in her town, and for Mary what had been *interest* in nuclear technology turned into concern, and then into activism. What followed was an intense crusade against the plant and its corporate and government supporters—a crusade that at times pitted Mary against almost everyone else in her community. But she persevered, and in 1984, at age sixty-five, she prevailed: Construction on the nuclear plant was stopped.

Mary is soft-spoken and intelligent, genteel in manner and appearance. She was born in Chisholm, Minnesota to parents who had immigrated from Austria-Hungary. Her father worked in the iron mines of northern Minnesota, where the lack of safety inspections led to frequent mining accidents. He was outspoken in politics and became one of the early labor organizers among his coworkers. There were six children; the family owned forty acres of land outside of town where they grew their own crops, which helped insulate them from the effects of the depression. "My mother did canning and made soups, and my father shot rabbits and deer, and that was how we made it through the depression," says Mary. "We never experienced the trauma of having nothing. It was a rigorous learning experience, not a defeat. I think going through that toughened me—plus watching my father stand up for what he thought was right."

Mary had a background in science that was unusual for a woman of her generation. She studied chemistry and English under a full scholarship at the College of St. Catherine in St. Paul, Minnesota, and later became a research librarian for the Dow Chemical Company in Midland. During World War II, she worked as an associate editor for *Chemical Industries* magazine in New York; after two and a half years she moved back to Midland, married Bill Sinclair, and took up technical writing for Dow. "I was paid low, 'women's wages,' but it was good experience; I got over any intimidation about complex documentation, and learned how to get through abstracts and summaries. I also learned how best to deal with technical information, which is to understand what you have to know to go forward, and to know your own limitations and where to go for help when you need it."

After the stint at the Library of Congress while her husband studied law, the Sinclairs moved back to Midland and started their family—having five children over eight years. Mary kept up with technical issues, and as the children grew up she turned again to her career, starting with freelance technical writing for Dow.

But she got sidetracked. In 1967, the local utility company, Consumers Power, announced plans to build a nuclear power plant in Midland, a mile from the main street downtown and two miles from Mary's home. The project was to consist of two nuclear reactor units; it was to cost almost $270 million and be completed in the mid-1970s. Dow Chemical, a powerful force in Midland because it employs one out of six of the city's residents, played a key role by contracting with the utility to buy power from one of the units. When the two companies teamed up to promote the plant to the community, Mary was appalled at the picture they painted. "It was the same line, about how safe, clean, and economical nuclear power would be. But I had been seeing in all the technical literature that a lot of the old problems with nuclear power hadn't been solved yet, and in fact, experts were identifying many more new ones that they hadn't even thought about before."

She was aware, for instance, that engineers both in the AEC and outside of government were calling attention to unresolved safety problems having to do with plant construction. Even a federal Advisory Committee on Reactor Safeguards had pointed out the urgent need for more safety research on certain aspects of the type of large-scale plants that were planned for Midland. There was also controversy raging within the AEC over health effects of exposure to the kinds of radiation that could be released either routinely or accidentally from nuclear plants. And no one had even begun to deal with problems of how and where to dispose of nuclear wastes from plants, which remain radioactive for hundreds of thousands of years.

But Mary still thought the problems could be solved. "I was still 'pronuclear' then," she explains. "I thought, sure we could make this technology work, but we would have to *work* to make it work. I knew we couldn't just accept advertising slogans in place of facing the real issues that had to be resolved. I decided that if our community was going to live that close to a nuclear plant, we should certainly be discussing the problems with the idea of solving them before the plant was completed. The issues were important ones that weren't just going to go away on their own. My whole point in raising them was to get the public concerned enough to stir up some action, either by congressional representatives or state officials, so that we could get a better handle on the problems."

She started writing letters to the editor of the *Midland Daily News,* in which she suggested "in the mildest terms" that there were problems to be discussed. The letters were published, but weren't received in the spirit she intended. She was surprised by the response. "I had simply taken what I thought was a routine action by a citizen," she says, "one I had seen as an obligation, since normally, if you live in a community and understand that something is wrong, you try to do something about it. The hostile reaction shocked me. People didn't like anything that constituted the least challenge to what Dow, Consumers Power, and the AEC were saying. They were a big power bloc; I knew that. I just hadn't realized *how* big."

The public was being told that Dow's coal-and oil-fired power plant was becoming obsolete, and that nuclear power was the only economical way to replace it. The implication was that without the new plant, Dow might take its operations elsewhere. As a result, people in the town felt threatened by Mary's challenge to the plant. "My social relationships just fell apart," she says. The newspaper printed derogatory letters about her, insinuating that she was a "know-nothing housewife." Editorials said she was stirring up needless controversy. People she knew avoided her on the street and in stores. "That's when I realized to what extent Midland was a company town," Mary says. "I had never been challenged like that before, or had my rights as a citizen, my freedom of speech, challenged. At that point I realized that my freedom of speech was as important to me as my concerns about nuclear power. I couldn't accept what I interpreted as repression of discussion of a legitimate public issue—one involving my family and home—and just walk away from it because I'd been pressured. Mentally, I shifted gears. I decided to study the issue more, in case I was missing something. Nuclear power is a very complex issue. I certainly didn't want to pursue my course if I was wrong. If I *was* mistaken, I'd be willing to stand corrected."

Mary has always been meticulous about having her facts straight. "Living in a community with a lot of Ph.D.s, most of whom were pronuclear power, I had to be very careful of credibility," she says. "I knew I wouldn't last a week if I wasn't absolutely sure of my data." As it turned out, though, facts weren't enough—something Mary attributes to a "cult of the atom and technology" that can't be penetrated with opposing facts. "I've learned that many corporate decisions aren't made on the basis of engineering or scientific data," she says, "but on the basis of what provides the best political advantage and profit."

In response to her public questions about the plant, the AEC and Consumers Power were sending Mary volumes of material, all of it pronuclear, and none of it really addressing the issues she had raised. Meanwhile, she attended a conference seminar in New York on nuclear power, featuring AEC representatives as well as scientists from major universities. Here she had the opportunity to hear information that wasn't "sanitized" by the AEC. She also learned that she wasn't alone in her concerns about nuclear power, but that citizens' groups were forming around the country on the issue, with many of the efforts being led by women. By the time she returned from the conference, she had resolved to pursue the matter in Midland.

There are two main stages in the process of building a nuclear power plant when citizens can raise objections, or intervene: in the beginning, when the utility applies to the government for a construction permit, and nearing completion, when the utility applies for an operating license. Citizen interventions in the proceedings are grueling, time-consuming, and expensive endeavors; they typically cost hundreds of thousands of dollars and involve reading and responding to mountains of extremely complex documents that require expert understanding of technical and legal nuances. Critics charge that the proceedings simply amount to collusion between the government and utilities. But Mary knew that citizen interventions are the only way to gain access to certain information about nuclear plants, and to see that the information gets to the public. She decided that if something was going to be done about the plant, it should be done at the construction licensing phase, rather than later when the plant was built. She thought the whole process might take her a year to eighteen months.

Mary began with a one-woman campaign to persuade her congressional representatives, the governor, and the state's Public Service Commission to face her questions. It was an exercise in futility. "Usually the first letter I'd get back would be 'Thank you for your interest, but we have complete confidence in the Atomic Energy Commission.' I'd then write back that they weren't addressing the technical issues, and would send materials to back up what I said. Gradually I found that copying and postage were using up the money I'd been saving to go to graduate school."

Mary also made copies of the best papers that she had gathered at the New York conference and sent them and other material to about twenty scientists she knew at Dow, with a cover letter to the effect that Midland was an intellectual, scientific community—didn't they agree that the community should discuss the issues she was raising, so that the safety of the plant would be better ensured? A couple of the scientists called her and said they realized she was right, but were afraid that to speak out might cost them their jobs. That was when Mary began forming a strong opinion of the powers of corporations to silence public debate. "I was amazed that this issue couldn't be discussed," she says. "Corporations diminish their own effectiveness by stifling discussion. Ignoring or subverting environmental concerns is something that isn't tolerated socially. These concerns get to be life and death issues with people, so they have to fight back."

Somehow—to this day, Mary isn't sure how—one of the packets she sent out made its way to Dorothy Dow Arbury, the eldest daughter of the Dow Corporation founder, Herbert H. Dow. Dorothy Dow turned up at Mary's door saying that she had her own concerns about the proposed plant and its connection to the Midland division of Dow. She asked Mary to send the material to the boards of directors of both Dow and Consumers Power, and offered to pay for the copying and postage, as well as for an initial effort to educate the community about the issues. She ended up providing financial help for the work over the course of several years. (Mary also estimates that she and her husband have spent some $100,000 of their own money on her work opposing the plant. What's more, after speaking out against it, she was "unemployable" in Midland, so it meant an additional cost in terms of lost salary.)

The mailing to Dow and Consumers Power received little response. "There were a couple of the same kind of letters, saying, 'Thank you for your interest; we have complete confidence in the AEC,'" Mary says. "I heard nothing at all from the Consumers Power board of directors—nothing." So she concentrated on informing the public. She was learning that she couldn't get any politicians to take a look at the situation in Midland unless a constituency was concerned about it. So in 1970 she formed the Saginaw Valley Nuclear Study Group, which eventually became an intervenor in the construction license hearings.

Apart from that small group, the hostility toward Mary hadn't subsided. She was still met with jeers and hisses when she tried to speak at other public forums. Because of the comments she'd elicit from people in public, she stopped going to the local symphony and for a while stopped attending her Catholic church. She received anonymous threatening phone calls and letters, and once had scraps of paper strewn on her lawn, with "Maoist" and "Communist" scribbled on them. Bill Sinclair's law practice began losing clients and his partner left. One morning the family woke to find an empty oil drum on the lawn, painted red, white, and blue, and labeled "atomic bomb." Mary wanted to get rid of it, but the children told her no, it was a "trophy." It's still in their garage. "The children sensed we were in a battle," Mary says. "That was an indication of their loyalty and fiery involvement."

Mary worried about her children being taunted at school. They were, but didn't tell her; they had made a pact among themselves—which she didn't learn about until years later—not to burden her with their troubles, since she was facing enough of her own. Dow and Consumers Power were by then building almost frenzied local support for the plant. A pronuclear rally was held in Midland in 1971 at which Art Linkletter joined with local residents in support of the plant's speedy licensing. The county commission undertook a $20,000 public relations campaign in favor of the plant, and Dow gave employees the day off to attend the rally. Practically all of Midland was a enthusiastic cheering section for nuclear energy.

It was at about this time that the newspaper editor wrote Mary to say that he had published enough of her views in the way of letters, and that she should take out advertising. For several months Mary's group documented the lopsided newspaper coverage of the plant, and then printed a booklet with the evidence. "All the paper was doing was turning the press releases of the utility and the AEC into articles, with photos of one local group giving another awards for supporting the plant, and articles about how such and such a committee had announced it supported nuclear power," she says. "All the while, there was serious repression of information critical of nuclear power."

After the booklet was published and distributed, Mary felt that coverage improved. Her group also complained to the Federal Communications Commission in Washington about local TV and radio coverage; the stations were applying for license renewals and they agreed to give the intervenors time to present their views.

The construction license hearings for the Midland plant ran from 1970 to the middle of 1972. Although the plant's supporters tended to blame the delays on the intervenors, in reality they were due to other things, not the least of which was the discovery of serious, industry-wide problems.

In 1971, for instance, it was learned (with no help from the AEC itself) that a series of important AEC tests in Idaho of nuclear power plants' emergency backup cooling systems had failed. (Nuclear plants are designed so that a conventional atomic explosion is impossible; the danger lies instead in intense overheating that could actually result in a plant's structure melting and its radioactive material leaking out. Nuclear plants therefore have elaborate cooling systems, and since 1967 the AEC had required backup emergency cooling systems. It was a series of computer-simulated tests of these systems that failed completely in late 1970.) The test failures were a serious blow to the nuclear industry, since it had been depending on the tests to prove that the emergency core cooling systems worked and that it was therefore safe to go on siting plants near large populations, as the industry and the AEC were doing in increasing numbers. In Midland, for instance, there were over 100,000 people living within a ten-mile radius of the proposed plant site. The AEC called for hearings in Washington to cover the new safety issues, and the Midland construction license hearings were recessed.

The problem with the emergency core cooling systems tests was by no means the only one plaguing the industry and its regulators. In 1969, two top AEC scientists working at the Lawrence Livermore Radiation Laboratory in California, John Gofman and Arthur Tamplin, had released results of a study that they had conducted on radiation effects. Their data showed that the effects could be far more serious than had been assumed previously, and they recommended that the AEC lower its standards for allowable radiation exposure by a factor of a least ten. The reaction against the two scientists, both within the AEC and from the industry, was intense. Their budgets and staffs were eventually cut so severely that they were forced to leave their jobs. Mary had followed the controversy around the scientists, and was particularly disturbed by the way they were treated. "It showed how people who spoke out or came up with unfavorable information about nuclear power were repressed, their budgets phased out, and their ability to work in their field extraordinarily limited," she says. Ironically, the AEC later came to see validity in the scientists' research, and lowered the radiation exposure standards to 1 percent of what they had been.

The nationwide nuclear problems slowed the Midland licensing process but didn't bring it to a halt. The national safety hearings disclosed serious problems with faulty testing and defective equipment, but in the end the AEC did nothing to stop plants from being built or from operating; instead it upgraded its safety standards somewhat. At the end of 1972, Consumers Power was granted the license to build its Midland plant.

Although the fight had already consumed several years of Mary's life, she wasn't ready to quit. "I realized how important this issue really was," she says. "It took a while for it to sink into my consciousness; at first, I was working on it simply because I thought certain facts needed to be confronted. I think it was the community's reaction that made me reconsider whether it was really worth going through the trouble. In a situation like that, you have to take a whole emotional and intellectual recapitulation of your convictions. The more I thought about it, the more I recognized the enormous implications of the development of nuclear power, the more clearly I saw that it wasn't just another technology. Having had five children at home so much of the time, my life and my decisions constantly revolved around them—what they were doing, what their future would be. I started seeing the nuclear issue in terms of them. The proliferation of nuclear power could profoundly affect their future; *they* were going to have to live with it, but it was our generation that was bringing it about. This realization shook my psyche.

"So what had started as just an opinion began to have huge implications. It started to fill my life; it became my motivation. I used to get up in the morning with a pain in my gut, thinking 'I've got to do something about the Atomic Energy Commission today—*something*.' I'd go jogging to work up the energy and determination to come home and get started. Gradually, I didn't have such a shock every morning; I just settled into living with the work."

Mary entered graduate school. Because of all the animosity she had encountered from people in the community—especially from highly educated people who hinted that she didn't know much, since she was, after all, "just a housewife"—she concentrated on courses related to her issue. She designed her own program at the University of Michigan, and in 1973 received her master's in environmental communications, now a popular program there.

She was to have plenty of opportunity to exercise the skills; for more than a decade she spent sixteen to eighteen hours a day, almost every day, working on the nuclear plant issue. She rarely took vacations. Studying legal documents and writing her own—often in round-the-clock stints to meet deadlines—became routine. Having lost the fight at the construction license stage, Mary and Myron Cherry, her group's attorney, decided to challenge the plant's license in the U.S. Court of Appeals for the District of Columbia Circuit, arguing that the environmental impact statement, required for the construction permit to be granted, was inadequate. Meanwhile, Mary was exhausting other channels as well. As the plant was being built, she carefully followed the documents on it, including inspection reports that disclosed evidence of shoddy construction work. In the mid-1970s, construction stopped altogether when the utility realized that some essential steel reinforcement rods had been misplaced or left out of one wall. Plant workers disclosed even more evidence of poor workmanship and of falsified inspection documents.

In the summer of 1976, Mary and her attorney won their appeal of the decision to grant the construction permit. The court agreed that the environmental impact statement had been inadequate, finding that among other things, it hadn't taken into account the effect of nuclear wastes on the environment, or considered conservation as an alternative to building the plant. The court ordered the Nuclear Regulatory Commission (which had taken over the regulatory functions of the AEC when the latter was abolished in 1975) to reconsider the decision to grant the permit. But instead of simply revoking the construction license and reopening the hearings on whether to grant a permit, the NRC held a separate set of hearings on whether or not to halt construction—while construction on the plant continued. Ultimately, the decision to let the utility go ahead was made by the U.S. Supreme Court; the utility appealed the lower court's ruling, and in 1978 the Supreme Court decided that construction could continue, in part because so much money had already been spent on the plant.

There was an important turn of events at the NRC suspension hearings that began in 1976, however. Documents subpoenaed for the hearings, and then testimony by Dow officials, showed for the first time that Dow was losing confidence in Consumers Power because of the construction delays and enormous costs. Dow, which could have built a new coal-fired plant, complete with pollution control equipment, for under $350 million, clearly would have liked to get out of the nuclear deal. But when the utility threatened to sue the company for the $600 million cost of the plant up until then, Dow buckled under the pressure and renegotiated its contract with Consumers Power.

Anyone with less stamina or weaker convictions might have given up in the face of these experiences, but Mary persisted. "You learn to be philosophical," she says. "And you keep discovering things when you stay in there working." One of the things she eventually found was that plant buildings were sinking and cracking because the soil on which they were being built hadn't been properly filled in and com- pacted. Eventually, as an intervenor in the operating license hearings for the plant, Mary presented eighteen "contentions," or reasons why the plant should not be permitted to operate.

Because of the unrelenting discoveries of new problems at the plant, public opinion in Midland gradually began to shift. By early 1983, as the *Midland Daily News* editorial noted, more people were realizing that Mary had been correct to raise objections to the plant. That February the NRC announced that it was fining Consumers Power $120,000 for major violations at the plant. A public meeting was held in Midland for the NRC and the utility to listen to public comments and answer questions. There was a huge crowd; micro- phones had to be set up in the halls for people who couldn't get in. Mary was accustomed to being booed when she spoke out at such gatherings; this time she was cheered.

Five months later, even Dow spoke out. When Consumers Power announced the new cost estimates for the plant—$4.43 billion, with a scheduled completion date of 1985—Dow backed out of its contract with the utility and filed a lawsuit to be freed of its contractual liabili- ties. Even with the plant's biggest customer lost and the powerful partnership between Consumers Power and Dow shattered, it still took more than a year before Consumers Power gave in. By then other industrial customers were worried about rate increases. In July 1984, the utility company finally dropped its plans for the plant. Since then, it has worked with Dow and other companies on converting the plant to a gas facility.

"I'd been waiting for this for so long, I didn't believe it at first," Mary says. "I thought the plant would be resurrected somehow. It hasn't happened, but for a long time there were still people here who were saying we needed that nuclear power." She began working on changing that view, going on radio and TV talk shows to address the issue of alternative sources of energy. She also began working with environmentalists on the problem of disposal of low-level radioactive wastes—another area where she feels the public has been misled—and on issues like researching better methods for reducing or detoxifying hazardous wastes.

The pressures of new missions don't compare with the pressure she felt fighting the nuclear plant. "There's nothing of the old tension now. I've established a certain credibility; I don't have to fight all over again for that. There was a lot of pain connected to my work on the plant at first, because of the hostility it generated. I know at times it was very hard on my husband too, though he never blamed me. Things were rough, but other things can make life rough, too, and at least he shared my concerns. We both felt this work of mine was just another part of parenting our children. In that sense, it made for an even greater bond between us.

"Doing this work, you have to dig in and avoid becoming bitter; you have to learn what love is in a scriptural sense, and practice it. It requires tremendous growth to continue, so you grow and change. If I had backed away from this challenge, I would never had had to reexamine my thinking, and my philosophical and spiritual life. To keep going—to keep remembering that it was ideas I was fighting, not people—I had to internalize passages in the scriptures, like the passage by Saint Paul, 'You can speak with the tongue of angels, but if you have not charity, it's like clanging cymbals.' There were other passages, too—favorites of mine that helped me live through times that were inscrutable to me."

"*Vociferous Residents*"

Cathy Hinds

6

"*The summary basically said that the state had conducted this health study because of issues raised by
an out-of-state researcher and a couple of vociferous
residents in East Gray. When Cheryl and I saw that,
we looked at each other and then got out the dictionary and looked up 'vociferous'—and found out
that it meant 'big mouth.'*"

*C*athy Hinds moved to the country so that her children could grow up in a healthy environment.

Cathy had been born and raised in Portland, Maine—a bustling city by that state's standards. She married young, and in 1975, when she was twenty-three years old, she left her job as an aide in a nursing home and moved with her family to the small town of Gray, in southern Maine just above Portland. Cathy had a three-year-old daughter, and was pregnant at the time; her second daughter was born three months after they moved. East Gray, where they settled in a little subdivision called Sundial Acres, was especially rural; many of the surrounding homes were farm houses, and some of Cathy's neighbors raised pigs or hens. "I wanted a quiet place with clean, fresh air," she says. "East Gray seemed ideal—out behind us there was even a farm with cows. It was just what a city girl would dream of for her kids."

There was something else in East Gray, too, that Cathy didn't know about. A quarter of a mile away from her new home was a hazardous waste dump.

Almost from the time she moved in, water was an issue in Cathy's new neighborhood. At first she wasn't concerned. "Being from the city, I had always thought that well water out in the country smelled funny. When I visited friends in the country and told them their water tasted or smelled strange, they'd explain that it was just the high iron content or manganese or something. So I figured that that must just be part of living in the country." In East Gray, Cathy's neighbor Cheryl Washburn, who had moved into the community earlier that year, told her that her own well water had such a bad odor that she couldn't drink it. Cheryl was hauling water in milk jugs from her mother's every day, and asked if she could start filling the jugs at Cathy's house instead. "I said sure, and thought, poor Cheryl, she's got that smelly well water stuff—iron or whatever." Another of the neighbors had also complained about the smell of his water, so the women reasoned that their neighbor's well and Cheryl's must have tapped into the same underground water supply. Cathy assumed that her well was different.

Cheryl had been hauling drinking water from Cathy's house for about a year when Cathy had a visit from an out-of-town friend, who commented on how terrible Cathy's water smelled. She hadn't even noticed it until then, but it started getting progressively worse, until people would come in and immediately notice the odor from the water throughout the house.

Smelly water wasn't Cathy's only problem. When she bathed her daughters, who were then going on two and five, they would cry and tell her the water was too hot, even though she tested it and knew that it wasn't. The girls developed skin rashes; Cathy had a doctor examine them but he couldn't explain what caused the rashes. And early in 1977, three months into another pregnancy, Cathy had a miscarriage. She had such serious bleeding problems that her doctor told her she should have a therapeutic abortion, but she miscarried before it was performed. The health problems got worse throughout 1977. Cathy's older daughter suffered from dizzy spells; sometimes she would be sitting at the dinner table and would get so dizzy that she would fall off the chair, or she would be walking and suddenly lose her balance and bump into furniture or walls. Cathy was very alarmed, but repeated trips to doctors and emergency rooms didn't yield any answers.

Cheryl's family was experiencing new health problems as well. She asked her doctor if the problems could have something to do with the water; he dismissed the idea and prescribed tranquilizers. But when the women started hearing other neighbors tell of problems, they arranged for meetings in various homes to talk about them. Cheryl contacted the city health officer, and invited him to the meetings. (The health officer was to become an important ally, but he got little support from other town officials; years later he was accused of embezzlement and, as Cathy puts it, "railroaded" out of town.)

The neighbors began exchanging stories about dizziness, headaches, and respiratory problems; they could see for themselves that many of them had similar rashes. The health officer took water samples and sent them out to various laboratories for testing. But the technology for testing water for a range of chemicals wasn't very advanced at that time, and months went by before a lab in Massachusetts finally identified three contaminants: the chemical compounds trichloroethylene, trichloroethane (both of which are toxic and potentially carcinogenic, or cancer-causing), and dimethyl sulfide. Eventually, dozens of contaminants were found in samplings of water in the neighborhood. Of the three chemicals identified initially, the dimethyl sulfide explained the odor in the water. "We later realized that we were lucky that there was something in there that caused the smell," Cathy says. "The other chemicals were odorless, and we might not have known for some time that something was wrong with the water—we could easily have been exposed a lot longer than we were."

Even as it was, the exposure went on longer than it should have. It turned out that not only were laboratories ill-prepared to handle the identification of contaminants—in addition, government health officials had very limited knowledge in the late 1970s about the health effects of chemical contaminants on the public. A state lab tested the water and told the residents that it was fit for drinking. But the local health officer started doing his own research on the chemicals, and whenever he discovered something new, he passed on the information to the residents. The revelations were gradual, over the course of several months. First Cathy and her neighbors received letters recommending that they not drink the water, since it could be harmful to their health. They stopped drinking it, but continued to use it for everything else. Next they learned that it wasn't safe for cooking—that contrary to what they first believed, and were led to believe, boiling didn't sterilize or break down the contaminants. The next round of advice was to avoid bathing in the water, but even then it was still considered safe for household use for cleaning, laundry, and flushing toilets. Finally, though, it became clear that even the fumes from the water were hazardous, and in January 1978 dozens of wells in the neighborhood were ordered capped.

Meanwhile, the health officer was trying to track down the source of the contamination. Since dimethyl sulfide was an agent used in natural gas, he had the pipeline inspected for leaks, but none were found. He then directed his attention to a waste recycling firm down the road from the homes, and testing revealed the same contaminants in water there. The McKin Company had been a small firm chiefly in the business of cleaning out fuel tanks until 1972, when it was awarded a contract to clean up an oil spill outside Portland harbor. Business picked up then, and the firm eventually handled wastes for some three hundred companies. Waste oils, including an array of toxic industrial chemicals, were collected in a pit and in barrels and underground storage tanks at the East Gray site. Cathy had noticed the McKin site, of course, but for some reason she had thought that it was involved in making tar for tennis courts. She had no idea that hazardous wastes were "disposed of" there or that contaminants were seeping into the acquifer, or underground water supply; neither had her neighbors or government officials. When the water contamination was linked to the site, the firm was ordered shut down—but the polluting chemicals remained.

Cathy's life was in upheaval. The health problems were a constant, daily concern. On top of her daughter's dizziness and her own headaches, Cathy's husband, who had never had respiratory problems before, developed severe asthma and on occasion had to be rushed to a clinic or hospital emergency room for treatment. The restricted use of the water added to the stress. When they stopped drinking the water in their homes, Cathy and Cheryl began going together to a public spigot at the town water district, loading their milk jugs there, and hauling them home—thirty jugs every other day. In the winter even that source was shut off and their only drinking water source was an outside spigot at the town office.

"There are some things that stand out more than others in my memories of those times," Cathy says, "and one of them is going with Cheryl in the dead of winter and filling our empty milk jugs. The water would run over our hands until we couldn't even feel them anymore. We'd get back into the car, and hold our hands over the defroster, and start crying like a couple of babies. The whole thing would just get to us—wondering about the kids, wondering what was going to happen to us. We were still seeing doctors, who were baffled and told us they didn't know what was wrong or what to do about our problems.

"My daughter started school in the fall of 1977, and all her new school clothes were ruined when I washed them in our water—black blotches that wouldn't come out. Then, when the wells were capped, the officials got funding to deliver town water to us, in seventeen-gallon civil defense barrels. It was going to be like having your dairy come around and deliver milk to your house. But after the first delivery, the health officer had that water tested, and found it had trichloroethylene in it too—and my husband and I panicked and wouldn't have anything to do with it. It was only trace levels, but on top of what we'd been exposed to, we didn't want it. So we asked if we could just have the barrels, and we kept putting clean liners in them and going to a different part of town—where there was a different water source—and filling them there.

"We were using the water in containers for everything by then; just to bathe my daughters I remember it took me exactly sixteen trips with four huge pans of water heated on the stove, and that put only about an inch of water in the tub! One time I was down to the very last bit of water in the barrel that we'd hauled. I heated it and put it in the sink to wash the dishes, but I hadn't put the plug in right, so it drained out. I sat down on the floor and cried. It might not sound like much to cry about, but when you're under that kind of pressure—well, all I could do was cry! But then I started getting smart. I got a dishpan, so I didn't have to worry about the plug; I'd heat the water and pour it in the dishpan, and then I realized the water wasn't too greasy, so I could use it to wash the floors. I'd do that, and then I'd use what was left for flushing the toilet."

The whole experience transformed Cathy, an otherwise reticent woman, into an outspoken advocate for her rights. She had always had a strong sense of right and wrong. "I guess I had it in me to do something when I saw things that were wrong—my parents instilled it in me. For them it was religious; my father is Baptist, and it was part of his sense of morality to say that if something's wrong, you should stand up and do something about it." When Cathy was working at the nursing home, she and a friend were appalled at some of the abuses they observed, including mental and physical mistreatment of patients. They wrote a report on the problems and gave it to the state agency that regulated nursing homes, which clamped down on some of the worst abuses.

In that case it was easy to know which agency to complain to; getting action at Gray was to be far more difficult. As soon as the contamination was discovered, the residents starting attending regular meetings, in which the town officials tried to figure out what to do about the water problem. "It almost seemed as though they were angry with us—as if we had done something wrong, and how dare we inconvenience them this way," says Cathy. "It was like talking to someone with no ears," Cheryl says. There were many meetings with state and local officials dickering about whose responsibility it was to help the neighborhood residents; later, federal officials entered the scene and merely joined in the dickering. At one early meeting where the officials were arguing among themselves, the residents felt that they were being treated as if they weren't even there. They were becoming increasingly frustrated. Cheryl had brought along a jar of her water, and at one point she and Cathy stood up with it and said, "We're going to make you drink this!" Then more and more people starting standing up in the room and demanding, "Drink the water! If you don't think anything's wrong with it, drink the water!" "They wouldn't have been able to get that water up to their noses, let alone drink it," says Cathy.

At another meeting, officials were trying to solve the question of how to haul clean water to the residents' houses. "Some official said they had an old gasoline truck that could be used, that they could clean it up—I couldn't believe they said that," says Cathy. "Then someone else said, no, there was a tank truck that could be used, but who would pay for the driver? I got so mad that I just stood up and said, '*I'll* drive the damn truck—I don't care who drives it as long as we get clean water!' " Cathy and Cheryl, meanwhile, were working as a team, going door to door in both the immediate neighborhood and the town of Gray, handing out fact sheets that they wrote up and copied, to inform people about what was going on and what the health officer was learning about the chemicals in the water, and to solicit public support. The effort paid off: When a public vote was finally taken on whether to extend the town water lines out to Cathy and Cheryl's neighborhood—which meant higher taxes for the whole town of Gray—the vote was unanimous. The wells had been capped in January 1978; that summer, the residents finally had clean water running in their homes again.

Cathy had become pregnant again. After some bleeding in the beginning, the pregnancy seemed to progress normally, and her doctor tried to assure her that the previous miscarriage had had nothing to do with her exposure to the contaminated water. In the eighth month of the pregnancy, though, the bleeding started again, and she delivered prematurely. Her son died two days later, on Christmas Day.

It wasn't until later that Cathy learned more about how her exposure to toxic chemicals could have been causing her problems. Among the chemicals in her water was benzene, which, experts told her, could account for the bleeding in her pregnancies. In that second pregnancy she apparently bled internally, so that a blood clot formed that bore down on the baby. She also learned that low birth weights are a common problem around hazardous waste dumpsites. Even though she had been in the eighth month of the pregnancy, her baby weighed only a little over one pound when he was born. "He had so many things wrong—liver problems, respiratory problems, kidney failure," she says. "He just didn't have a chance."

Meanwhile in 1978, the country began to learn about the consequences of decades of unregulated dumping of toxic chemicals, as the story of Love Canal unfolded. Love Canal was an abandoned waterway in the city of Niagara Falls, New York, where the Hooker Chemical Company had dumped over twenty thousand tons of toxic chemical wastes. In the early 1950s, Hooker filled up the canal, covered it with dirt, and turned the site over to the local board of education. Homes went up around the area, and a school was built near a corner of the canal. Residents complained of health problems as early as the 1950s, but it wasn't until the late 1970s that state and federal officials began conducting health studies in the area. The rate of miscarriages, still-births, and birth defects in the area was unusually high, and an abnormally high rate of chromosome damage—which can lead to cancer or genetic damage—was found in area residents. Eventually several thousand families were evacuated from the neighborhood.

In early 1979, Cathy and Cheryl watched a television documentary, "The Killing Ground," which covered the Love Canal tragedy and other toxic waste problems around the country. Suddenly they knew they weren't alone. "I was so relieved," says Cathy. "Not to see others suffering, but to realize that there was someone else we could talk to about this who would know what we were talking about, who would understand how we felt. The officials didn't understand; even our friends didn't know what hell and terror we were going through." That month Cathy ran her telephone bill up to six hundred dollars. She called everyone she could who was portrayed on the film, including Lois Gibbs, the woman who had organized her Love Canal neighbors and helped form the Love Canal Homeowners Association to make sure that residents were treated fairly by state and federal officials.

Seeing the documentary and talking to other people around the country gave Cathy the impetus she needed to step up her own activity at Gray. She and Cheryl had unwittingly been using organizers' tools already, including talking to the press about their water problems and going door-to-door in the town to get information to people. They now decided that an organization would lend more credibility to their efforts, and together formed the Environmental Public Interest Coalition, or EPIC. The group had about twenty members, including neighbors from East Gray as well as people from different parts of the state who had seen Cathy and Cheryl on the news and had sought their advice because of their own concerns about water contamination. The small size of the group was a well-kept secret; on several occasions, it became evident to Cathy that state environmental officials assumed that EPIC had many more members than it had, a misconception that she manipulated to the group's advantage. "We never lied to officials about our members, but it was convenient to let them believe what they wanted to believe!"

Because of her experience in Gray, Cathy was being invited regularly to testify before state legislative committees that were considering new environmental legislation. Not long after her baby was born prematurely, she was asked to testify in favor of a new law that would require the state government's regulation and monitoring of toxic chemicals at each stage, from production through disposal. "I started telling my story, but it was so soon after the death of my son, and I hadn't talked about it publicly until then," she says. "I sat there, with the committee looking down on me, and the room packed with people, and I broke down crying. Part of me wanted to turn around and run out, but somehow I kept going, and left as soon as I was finished." Later someone called her at home to tell her that that was the fastest they had ever pushed a bill through committee.

Until then, no official health studies had been conducted on the neighborhood residents to learn of any potential long-term health problems. The Gray health officer had proposed such a study earlier, but the state had refused to fund it. In 1979 both Cathy and a state health consultant who had heard her testify, separately contacted Beverly Paigen, a cancer research scientist from Buffalo, New York, who had been working with the people around Love Canal. She offered to travel to Gray to learn about the site and talk to the residents. With the immediate problem of supplying residents with safe drinking water finally out of the way, local and state officials had begun to focus on the site itself. When the firm was closed, it had been ordered to do some excavation work to remove contaminants, but that work had not been done, and the state itself had come in and hired a trucker to haul away the aboveground liquid contaminants. By August 1979, Cathy had received a letter from the state Department of Environmental Protection assuring her that the aboveground liquids had been removed. But Cathy was already learning to be skeptical about officials' promises. When residents took Beverly Paigen to the site, they discovered barrels with liquids in the nearby woods, as well as onsite tanks containing some liquids. The fumes were very strong. There were children playing on the site; one child was trying to pry open the cover to an underground storage tank. Graffiti on buildings and tanks, as well as bike tracks in the soil, made it clear that children played there regularly.

Cathy and Cheryl were so upset by what they found that they initiated their own press conference. They had recognized the value of talking to reporters, but until then reporters had always called *them*. When the reporters from TV stations, radio stations, and newspapers gathered at Cathy's front porch, Cathy realized she didn't even know how a press conference was conducted. She looked at them and asked, "How do I do this?" Someone prompted her to simply say what she wanted to tell them. So she held up the letter in which the state claimed that the aboveground liquid contaminants had been removed from the site, and described what they had discovered with Beverly Paigen. The next morning, a state official was at her door. Cathy immediately contacted reporters, and went with the official to the site and demanded that the liquids be removed, the fence around the site repaired and the site completely closed off, with any offsite barrels or tanks moved into the fenced area.

What happened next was completely spontaneous on Cathy's part. The official asked when Cathy's group expected the work to be done. She quickly replied, "Within two weeks." The official said that would be impossible—that maybe it could be completed within two months. That was unacceptable, Cathy said, and warned him that if the state didn't do it, members of EPIC would go onto the site and do the work themselves. "At that point I could imagine what he was thinking— hundreds of members of EPIC down there, with the press looking on! So when we left, I figured we'd better cover ourselves, and we got on the phone to find people who would be willing to go onsite if that's what it came to. We called around and found some gas masks; we even called the lawyer for the owner of the site for permission to enter the site if we needed to.

"The day before the two weeks were up, the official called back and said, 'Cathy, I know it would be hard for you to reach all your members, but maybe you can get a quorum vote at least, to give us some more time on this.' And I said, 'Oh, that's going to be impossible. I don't think I can even talk to them at this point—they're all so furious about this whole thing, and they're ready to go in there if you're not there tomorrow!' Sure enough, the next day workers were at the site doing what we had demanded. So it was reinforced in our minds—adding to the education we were getting at that time—that the press was one of our best tools for pressuring officials to get things done."

Humor was important, too. "We had to keep our sense of humor, or we'd have gone crazy," Cheryl says. "Even naming the organization was funny—before we came up with EPIC, we had thought of the name 'Environment Near Death,' or 'END.' But then we pictured it in the papers, and thought of 'The END is coming!' and realized we really had to change it, or people would think we were some far-out religious group!"

Beverly Paigen followed up her visit to Gray with a letter to state officials, warning that the health complaints she heard of in East Gray were similar to health problems at Love Canal, and recommending that a health study be undertaken of area residents and that air sampling be conducted. She expressed concern that even though residents were no longer using contaminated well water, chemicals could be seeping into the soil and into the air in basements and homes, and that the contamination could eventually spread to a nearby acquifer and into a river flowing through other communities. During her visit, she had examined documents that Cathy had on hand, including results of water testing, and had determined that when residents were still using well water, trichloroethylene levels in their homes were thirty times higher than the levels had been in Love Canal homes.

The state did conduct air sampling in the homes and discovered contamination, but assured the residents that it was normal to have those chemicals in homes and pointed out that the levels found were within federal standards. "That taught me another important lesson— that something was wrong with the standards," Cathy says. The state also undertook a health study of the residents. An epidemiologist assigned to the state by the federal Centers for Disease Control conducted the study; sessions were scheduled for residents to have blood drawn and to bring in urine samples. Almost immediately Cathy knew that she couldn't have much faith in the the study. While the epidemiologist was drawing blood from one resident's arm, a reporter asked him what he expected to find; his reply was "nothing." Cathy wasn't surprised, then, when the study results were released, declaring that no serious health problems existed. "The summary basically said that the state had conducted this health study because of issues raised by an out-of-state researcher and a couple of vociferous residents in East Gray. When Cheryl and I saw that, we looked at each other and then got out the dictionary and looked up 'vociferous'—and found out that it meant 'big mouth.' "

The study was to be faulted by several experts, including Beverly Paigen, who pointed out that although there didn't appear to be persistent health problems in the neighborhood, the study was conducted a year and a half after the direct exposure to contamination had ceased, and that symptoms of disease—though not not necessarily disease itself—could fade in as little as four months. She recommended that the residents be monitored regularly for long-term health problems, and that environmental tests be conducted to determine the exact extent of the contamination. And she put in a word for the women, noting that often the first alert of hazardous waste pollution in a community was through women talking among themselves about reproductive and other health problems. "Thank God for the vociferous residents," she told one newspaper.

Cathy's activism was taking a toll on her private life. "We were still attending meetings regularly," she says. "If one of the larger environmental groups in the state had a meeting, I would go; if the Department of Environmental Protection had a meeting, I would go. I ate, drank, slept this issue of hazardous wastes. Every move I made was dictated by it. It was a very difficult time for my family—everything suffered because of my involvement. My housework suffered; my relationship with my husband suffered—later we were able to resolve things better, to find a middle ground. But during that time I was always tired or upset; the children rarely got to see me. I was in constant communication with the contacts I had made around the country after 'The Killing Ground.' I continued to accept invitations to speak around the state before college classes and civic groups, because I thought it was important to spread the word. I knew that the level of public awareness on the issue was low; people had no idea of the personal side of living near a dumpsite. We had also initiated a lawsuit against the owner of the site in 1977, but that seemed to be going nowhere, because it was the first lawsuit of its kind." (The suit was eventually settled out of court.)

At one point Cathy was invited to speak about her experiences at Gray before a class at the University of Maine. After telling her story, she learned that the class was studying victims of hazardous waste pollution to see how their experiences related to the "post-distress" syndrome suffered by other victims, including Vietnam War veterans. They explained to her that eventually the victim can do one of two things—withdraw, or become an activist and fight back. "I could see it in my own family, with me and my husband," Cathy says. "After our baby son died, he didn't want to hear about the problem any more. It was too painful for him to deal with, so he put it out of his head. That was his reaction. Mine was that I was mad, and I was going to do something about it." Eventually Cheryl was to withdraw from the issue as well; she and Cathy have remained close friends, and she supports Cathy's continued involvement. "We were just under so much stress that whole time," Cheryl says. "It takes a certain person to be able to keep at it all the time. Cathy is one of those people. She's strong, and in some ways strong willed. For me, it came down to wanting to live a normal life. I didn't want to be faced with this thing every day, or I'd be a basket case. I didn't want to go to all the meetings, to keep butting my head against a wall. As Cathy slowly started doing more, I slowly backed off. Cathy has a way with words—she knows how to put things, and I was glad to let her take over. I'm proud of what we did—and I'm proud of her for keeping it up."

In 1980 Cathy became pregnant again, and was very worried about the pregnancy. She had a new doctor, and made her past medical records available to him; he had her blood checked for genetic problems, and had ultrasound tests done regularly to check on the growth of the baby and the placement of the placenta. "I felt fairly safe with this doctor," she says. "He saved my sanity during that time. I just waited for the baby to be born, and prayed that everything would be alright." Her son Joshua was born in March 1981. At first he seemed healthy, but shortly after she brought him home, he developed jaundice. She stopped nursing him and for a while his health improved.

Cathy was still concerned about the air in the homes being a possible contamination route. A woman who had recently moved into one of the nearby homes contacted Cathy; she had heard about the health problems and wanted to know more about what had happened in the community. She raised Siamese cats, and kittens were being born deformed. "We had gone through that earlier, with our cats having deformed or stillborn kittens," says Cathy. "When I saw that it was still happening, after the town water was brought in and some remedial measures had been taken at the site, I became very scared. We called a press conference and showed the deformed cats to the press. I told a state health department official that they should come in and test the air again—his response was to ask how it would benefit the department!

"That's when I knew I wanted to move. I didn't care if we had to move into a shack as long as I got out of Gray. I was still committed to doing what I could about the problems, but I wanted to get out for my family's sake. It hit home even more when my baby became very ill and had to be hospitalized, and I learned that his liver function tests were abnormal."

They put the house up for sale. But at the end of 1981, before the house was sold, Cathy received another alarming piece of information. By this time, she had developed sympathetic contacts within state agencies—people who would quietly supply her with information that they picked up about the site. Someone gave her a copy of a previously unreleased report that had been prepared for the federal Environmental Protection Agency, as part of the EPA's planning work under the new federal "Superfund" law, which provided money for cleaning up the most dangerous hazardous waste sites in the country. The report disclosed that at one point state testing had found the cancer-causing chemical polychlorinated biphenyls, or PCBs, at the site, and also warned that the geology of the area around Gray was such that pollution could be affecting the nearby Royal River. The study also criticized the previous health study of the residents as subjective and limited.

Cathy was faced with a dilemma. She was trying to sell her house and move away. That summer, the McKin site had been passed up for federal Superfund cleanup money; instead, another site, in Winthrop, Maine, was chosen by state officials as the site in the state most in need of the federal money. "We were in a lull period—things had calmed down and there wasn't much press about McKin, so we were thinking we should sell the house and get out of there while we could. Then I had a massive attack of conscience—I realized that I couldn't sell the place without telling people what I knew. Here I had been going on about the problem all these years, and now I had this new information, and didn't know what to do with it. I called Lois Gibbs for advice, and all she could tell me was that it was a 'catch-22' situation, and that I had to do what I thought was right. I stayed up all night worrying, and then I called the press. The 'for sale' sign was right there on my front lawn when the reporters came over to look at the report."

The release of the report helped stir up enough public pressure to eventually force the EPA to put the McKin site on the Superfund list; the site was to be ranked among the worst 8 percent of such sites around the country. Cathy's house was sold anyway. She saw to it that the buyers knew the history of the area—"I had a file cabinet in the kitchen; I opened up the drawers, gave them some coffee, and told them they should go through everything in there." Cathy and her family moved in May 1982 to New Gloucester, a community just north of Gray. Shortly after they moved, her son had a seizure and was checked for epilepsy—but then suddenly the problems stopped. "Seven months after we moved into our house, everything was better. Joshua's liver tests were normal. There were no more seizures. My husband's asthma was gone. We get recurring rashes every year, and don't know if there's a connection to what happened at Gray—but basically the health problems we had had were gone."

Cathy didn't declare victory for herself and her family and start taking it easy—instead, she broadened her involvement. She had developed into an expert on the issue of toxic wastes, or "toxics," and was respected by the press as articulate and reliable. She continued to work locally on the McKin site, but also got involved with organizations on a statewide, and then national, level. She cofounded the Maine Citizens Coalition on Toxics, which later became part of an existing statewide citizens group, the Maine People's Alliance. Through her work in Maine she met an organizer with the National Campaign Against Toxic Hazards and became very active with that organization's lively lobbying campaign for the renewal and strengthening of the federal Superfund law, which meant several trips to Washington to meet with members of Congress and EPA officials. More important, the effort brought her together with other hazardous waste site victims from around the country. "I was so pleased to find an organization bringing people together like that; way back in 1979, Cheryl and I had been thinking along those lines—that a national group should be formed—when we first started contacting the people we saw in 'The Killing Ground.'"

In 1987, Cathy joined the group's staff as an organizer. At that point, there were nearly one thousand Superfund sites around the country; the federal Office of Technology Assessment had estimated that some ten thousand toxic dumpsites would eventually need to be cleaned up.

The Superfund law that was finally reauthorized in the fall of 1986 contained many of the provisions the National Campaign lobbied for, including increased funding, and schedules and strict standards for cleaning up sites. While she was lobbying for the Superfund improvements, Cathy was learning firsthand, through her continued involvement with the McKin site, why the changes in the law were so important. It took constant vigilance and public pressure to ensure that the cleanup plans for the site were adequate. One of the EPA's first proposals for cleaning up the dump, for instance, called for simply plowing up successive layers of soil and exposing them to the air, so that the chemicals could evaporate. The residents were outraged that after they had been exposed to poisons in their drinking water, the government was proposing to subject them to the same chemicals in their air. Cathy helped organize a demonstration against the plan—complete with a bubble machine to show graphically how the contaminants would float into the air.

As is usual at Superfund sites, at McKin the EPA negotiated with the private companies that were identified as being chiefly responsible for the toxic contamination, and came up with a cleanup agreement. With technical assistance from Henry Cole, a former EPA scientist who became research director for the National Campaign Against Toxic Hazards, Cathy scrutinized the McKin cleanup plans, worked for improvements, and demanded that adequate monitoring be conducted around the site to determine whether chemicals were escaping into the air. "I had learned early on not to trust officials—we had had trouble with them at every level," says Cathy. "I try to work within the system, but when there's trouble, I know now how to hold them accountable. With the McKin plans, we were watching them all the time, on issues like the cleanup itself, as well as where the air monitors should go, how many there should be, how often they would be read. We nailed them whenever we saw something wrong. And if they didn't listen, we called a press conference right at the site and made a big stink." The cleanup plan that was finally approved at McKin involved a completely closed system—still not the ideal method, according to Henry Cole, but vastly improved over the original plan. Cleanup of the site finally began in 1986.

Henry Cole has worked closely with activists around the country on the issue of toxics. "There are a lot of people working on this issue who started out as ordinary people going about their ordinary lives, and then experienced a sudden, drastic change when they were confronted with the knowledge that there was a dump nearby," he says. "You see all kinds of responses in people. There are maybe a couple hundred people around the country—largely women—whose response has been to turn the pain and anger and fear into a very constructive working for solutions. A few of these women move away from the site, but continue to be active on that site and others; they begin to see the bigger picture. These women seem to instinctively understand what organizing is about, how to move people and organize people; they're in a class by themselves.

"Cathy is one of them. In her case, added to these other qualities is an extraordinary spiritual integrity. She's not in the least bit cynical—which is a remarkable thing in a human being who's gone through what she has. More than anyone I've met, Cathy has a spiritual strength to deal with this problem, and it spills over to others—she's able to move people. She's not naive. She knows how companies abuse their power, how her government is spineless and covers things up. But skepticism is very different from cynicism, and something spiritual in her prevents her from being cynical. Instead of throwing her hands up, she knows there's something deeply worth fighting for. She's a source of inspiration to me. I look at a lot of numbers and reports, and they become abstract without the human connection. Cathy has played an enormously important role in making that connection, not just in Gray but around the country."

At a conference held in New Hampshire in 1984, to kick off the Superfund lobbying effort, Cathy was reminded of why she has remained involved in the toxics issue. "Officials from the EPA were there," she says. "There were a thousand people in the audience, and microphones had been set up all around. People lined up at those microphones for hours just to get a chance to talk to the EPA about their sites. And just the way the memory of Cheryl and me sitting in the car holding our hands over the defroster is forever etched in my mind, I'll always remember the image of this little boy waiting in line at one of the microphones. When his turn came, he pushed a chair up to the microphone and stood on it, and gave his name and said, 'I'm eight years old, and I have leukemia. I want to know how come you aren't doing something about the problem in my neighborhood.' He said friends of his had leukemia too, and then looked at the EPA officials and said, 'I don't want to die.' That boy, and the loss of my own first baby son, and hearing all the other stories of people like us around the country—all that's been a fuel to me. It makes me think that, damn it, this is *America,* this stuff shouldn't be happening, and I'm not going to sit back and let it happen. I want to be part of fighting to do something about it."

"Common Sense"

Alice Weinstein
and
Marion Weisfelner

"It's a matter of common sense. You don't have to be an engineer to know that so many people simply could not have made the same mistake. We certainly couldn't all be so stupid as to have to be taught how to use the gas and brake pedals, and how to sit in our cars!"

Alice Weinstein became an activist the day the car she was driving plowed into a neighbor's tree.

Her car had been parked in her neighbor's circular driveway; Alice climbed in and turned on the engine, but when she shifted from "park" into "drive," the automobile shot out of control, across the lawn and into a tree. Both Alice and her daughter, who was home from college and sitting next to her in the front seat, were thrown against the windshield. Her daughter's front teeth were chipped; Alice had to have stitches and plastic surgery on her face.

Alice had had trouble once before with the car, a 1982 Audi 5000. Eleven months earlier, she had had a similar accident, when she backed the car out of her driveway and it suddenly bolted across the street into a snowbank. Alice wasn't hurt, and when she eased the car out of the snow, it seemed to be operating normally. She was upset, though, and took the auto into her Audi dealer for an inspection. He looked it over, assured her he couldn't find anything wrong, and explained that she must have had her foot on the accelerator instead of the brake. Alice knew that that wasn't the case, but even her husband didn't believe her. When the accident happened again, this time with their daughter as witness to the fact that Alice's foot was firmly on the brake pedal, her husband came around.

Until then, Alice's only crusading had been for animal rights. She lives in a comfortable suburban Long Island, New York neighborhood and runs a mail order stationery business; her husband commutes to work at his printing company in Manhattan. Except for letters to legislators on animal rights issues, Alice says she was never politically involved. But now she was to become active in a new and very different crusade—one that would pit her against an automobile manufacturer and the federal government.

It began with talking. Alice describes herself as a "talker," and she talked about her accident a lot. The first evening, through friends of her daughter, Alice heard of someone else who had had a similar accident. She got on the phone, and within hours she had the names of five people whose Audis had shot out of control in the same way, when they were shifting from "park" to "drive" or "reverse." And over the next months, she kept finding more. "I was walking around with my face in a cast for a while, and I almost always ended up talking to people about the accident. I didn't let up for a minute—at cocktail parties, at my son's soccer games or little league games, walking through the supermarket. If I happened to see an Audi in a parking lot, I'd get obsessed. I used to be known as the 'dog lady' in the neighborhood because I was always rescuing dogs. Now people started calling me the 'Audi lady.' "

And it seemed that everywhere she went, she came home with the name of someone else who had had the same kind of accident. By the time Alice met Marion Weisfelner, she knew of dozens of people who had had sudden acceleration accidents in their Audi 5000s.

Marion was taking her mother home to her apartment building when the accident happened. She pulled her 1985 Audi 5000 into the driveway in front of the building, let her mother out at the lobby, and unloaded some groceries. She was going to park the car and go upstairs with her mother. But when she got into the car, turned on the engine, and shifted into "reverse," the car sped off backwards, down the driveway, onto the lawn, and into a tree. Marion wasn't hurt—just astounded. "I'm a very honest person. If I had done something wrong, I'd be the first to admit it. And if I had put my foot on the wrong pedal, I'd have known it. But I didn't do anything wrong. I told the police just how it happened—it was as if the car was possessed! There was a woman sitting in the car parked next to me; I was going to take her parking spot. As she described it, one second I was there, and then I wasn't there—she said it was like an apparition. I was just lucky that I wasn't hurt, or that no one happened to be walking behind the car."

Marion's husband runs a dry cleaning shop, and she phoned him immediately from her mother's apartment. A customer was in the shop and overheard the conversation. He didn't mention anything at the time, but a few days later he came in again, this time with Alice's phone number. "My husband called me up from the shop, all excited," says Marion. "He said, 'You're not going to believe this, but other people have had the same accident as yours!' That's when I realized my husband hadn't believed that I didn't cause the accident. He'd been very sympathetic, and in the four days since the accident he'd never once told me that he thought it was my fault. But the sound of relief in his voice was so obvious, when he told me it was happening to other people, that I suddenly knew he hadn't believed me." Marion had been on the telephone for the better part of two days battling with Audi, whose dealers and officials told her repeatedly and emphatically that they'd never heard of that kind of accident happening with the car. The truth was something else entirely, as she was to learn from Alice.

Marion and Alice met, hit it off right away, and quickly became partners in trying to get the bottom of the Audi problem. They live just ten minutes apart, and Alice's office is across the street from Marion's husband's dry cleaning shop, where Marion works part time. So the two of them found it very convenient to start working together, making calls to Audi dealers, consumer hotlines, and other Audi drivers who had had accidents to get more details. "It turned out that the first five people on my list all live in the same area and had bought their car from the same dealer, who told every one of them that he'd never heard of that problem happening before," says Alice. "And that was just the beginning."

After a series of fruitless phone calls, Alice and Marion finally happened on the Center for Auto Safety, a Washington, D.C.-based private consumer advocacy group. Alice spoke to a staff person there, Dan Howell. "When something like this happens, you have no idea where to start, whom to call," she says. "I didn't even know there was a federal agency responsible for car safety. We must have tried ten different agencies before one of them referred us to the Center for Auto Safety. It was such a relief—Dan was the first person I spoke to about my accident who didn't ask me if my foot had been on the accelerator." She told him of the others who had had accidents; it turned out that his organization had been following the problem for some time and had its own long list of people who had called with similar complaints. "From there, it snowballed," she says.

Dan Howell put the women in touch with the New York Public Interest Research Group, a statewide consumer organization whose director, Tom Wathen, started to teach them the rudiments of a full-scale consumer fight against a manufacturer. Within a couple of weeks, in March 1986, the New York State Attorney General joined them in petitioning the National Highway Traffic Safety Administration, an arm of the federal Department of Transportation, to order a recall of the car. NHTSA has the power to investigate automobile defects and to require manufacturers to recall and repair defective cars.

But groups like the Center for Auto Safety charged that under the Reagan administration, NHTSA had become reluctant to spar with auto manufacturers, and that the number of defect investigations and recalls had dropped dramatically from pre-Reagan levels.

NHTSA already had a low-level investigation under way into the Audi problem, in addition to separate investigations into sudden acceleration defects in several other automobile models (the incidence rate of accidents in the Audi 5000—about one in every three hundred cars—was much higher than in any other car being investigated). While the NHTSA investigation dragged on, Audi never budged from its argument that the problem was the fault of the driver, not the car. Still, it had received enough complaints by 1982 and 1983 to warrant conducting two voluntary recalls of early models—both of them designed simply to reduce the likelihood that a driver could mistakenly hit the wrong pedal. In one case, the recall was to make adjustments on floor mats, so that they wouldn't interfere with the accelerator and brake pedals; the other recall was to raise the brake pedal and widen the space between it and the accelerator. Meanwhile, on a case-by-case basis, Audi was often quietly buying back cars that had been in accidents and paying for property damage, or letting customers out of lease arrangements. Marion was reimbursed in full by Audi for her car; Alice received an insurance settlement.

The attorney general's involvement in the Audi issue brought a surge of television and newspaper coverage—and with the publicity, calls started pouring in to Marion and Alice with more and more accounts of accidents. In her public statement at a news conference announcing the recall petition, Alice warned that it was just a matter of time before someone would be killed because of the defect. What she didn't know was that such an accident had already occurred; in Ohio a month earlier, a six-year-old boy had been opening the garage door when the family car, driven by his mother, surged out of control and crushed him to death.

Alice and Marion were keeping a computerized list in Marion's home of the people who had complained of Audi accidents, and a few weeks after the press conference, they got together a group for a meeting to decide how to fight back against Audi. The room was packed that night, and the group decided to band together in the "Audi Victims Network," with the goal of either getting the car off the road or forcing a recall for repairs to correct the problem once and for all. Alice and Marion were chosen to be president and vice president of the new organization.

Their lives were consumed with the Audi issue. Every day, they would receive at least one or two phone calls with new reports of sudden acceleration accidents in the Audi. One woman who called had been dropping off a friend when her car surged forward and hit the friend, who was in the hospital in a coma as a result. The woman was so upset that she phoned a crisis intervention center, and was referred to Alice and Marion. "We really ended up providing counseling to people," says Marion. "It's horrible enough to have one of these accidents, but it's much worse when people tell you it's your fault." "If we accomplish nothing else," Alice says, "at least we can let people know they aren't to blame."

Besides answering calls from people with reports of accidents, and making calls to Audi and NHTSA to follow up on what they were doing about the defect, Marion and Alice began distributing leaflets on streets and in parking lots—wherever they saw the car parked— warning Audi drivers of the possibility that their car had a potentially deadly defect. The Audi 5000 is an expensive car, selling for over $20,000, and Long Island and the New York City area make up a significant part of the Audi market. Some owners didn't want to listen to Alice and Marion's warning. "People can be very sensitive about their cars, believing that their cars reflect on them," Alice says. "With an automobile like the Audi, they've made an expensive purchase, and don't want to be told that their choice was a mistake." Other people wondered why Alice and Marion continued to be involved in the issue—since they weren't driving Audis any longer themselves. "I won't set foot in an Audi again," Alice says, "but that doesn't mean I can't be hurt by one. The people who are hurt most often are people who happen to be in the path of one when it goes beserk, and this car goes beserk in busy places—places like shopping centers, drive-in banks, gas stations."

Audi felt pressured enough by the publicity and the haranguing from the victims' group to agree to a meeting with them in May 1986. It was the first time the company had ever met that way with a group of consumers, and Alice and Marion and the other members of the victims' network felt heartened. They were to be disappointed, though. The Audi officials came to the meeting with a prepared report on the company's own study of the defect, in which it claimed essentially what it had insisted all along: that it could find nothing wrong with the car, and that the accidents had been caused by mistakes on the drivers' parts, not by any defect in the Audi. Most of the accidents it had studied, the company said, had happened to inexperienced drivers who were under five feet five inches tall—the implication being that the accident happened mostly to women drivers. At the meeting, the Audi officials announced yet another repair that would be made to the car, replacing the brake and accelerator pedals; the company said it was also making available to drivers a free cassette to "reacquaint" them with proper seating positions and driving controls.

The group was enraged. "It's a matter of common sense," says Alice. "You don't have to be an engineer to know that so many people simply could not have made the same mistake. It was as if we had all gotten together and agreed on our story; the language people used to describe the accident was always the same—the car 'bolted,' it 'flew,' it was 'possessed.' We couldn't all be wrong—and we certainly couldn't all be so stupid as to have to be taught how to use the gas and brake pedals, and how to sit in our cars!"

They weren't getting much action from the government, either. By the summer, there had been over five hundred reports of Audi sudden acceleration accidents, with at least four deaths. NHTSA stepped up its investigation into the car one notch, but stopped short of ordering a recall or even opening a full-scale investigation. Alice and Marion kept up the pressure, constantly badgering NHTSA officials to see what they were doing, and sending in any reports of accidents that they received. "In the beginning NHTSA actually asked us to stop flooding them with accident reports, because they'd just have more paperwork to do," Alice says. "Then they started saying every accident was important, and to keep handing them in. We had kept it up anyway. But the time they were taking! If there's a defect out there that's killing people, you'd think they'd be able to move more quickly on it!"

"I used to think that the government did what it's supposed to to protect people," says Marion. "But I was learning that the government does whatever you *allow* it to." "It's been an education," says Alice. "The U.S. may have some of the best auto safety laws; in Europe they don't do the same kind of defect investigations. But every time we got somewhere with the government on this problem, we realized there was still another obstacle to confront. And I started learning things; when you trace the history of the auto industry and government, you realize how bad the record really is. There was the defect in Fords several years back—parked cars would slip out of 'park' into 'reverse,' and roll out of control. The injuries were even worse than with the Audi, because there were so many of the cars sold, and the accidents would happen when the driver wasn't even in the car. All the government ended up doing in that case was requiring a little warning sticker on the inside of the car. There was a defect that could have been corrected, but maybe Ford would have gone out of business, and the government didn't want that on its hands. And there are so many other cases that have been dropped. It's scary, really."

Alice and Marion persevered—taking calls from Audi owners, getting out mailings to the group, talking to reporters, keeping after Audi and government officials. "Our lives were turned upside down," says Marion. "You could walk into either of our houses and know we did not lead normal lives anymore. Everything functioned—the kids weren't going around hungry or without clothes—but sometimes it was total chaos. And yet you still do it; you can't stop, because you believe strongly in what you're doing."

Audi was feeling the effects of the bad publicity. Sales were down in the New York area, some parking garages wouldn't allow Audi 5000s to be parked there, and a few insurance companies stopped insuring the car. Some of the Audi dealers began blaming Alice and Marion. "We were called 'the two bitches on Long Island,' " says Marion. "Or," says Alice, "'those middle-aged Jewish women.' " If the name-calling didn't rankle them, the implication that the accidents were the fault of women drivers did. "I'm a different person because of this fight," says Alice. "I'm more interested in women's rights than I was before. I had never felt that I had to prove myself as a woman—in my family, my mother is a lawyer, my sister is a lawyer, and women have always been respected. But I see that we still have a lot to combat outside our own circles. Here we had Audi singling out women for the blame. And I found that even if you're just calling to complain about something—if a woman calls and complains, that's one thing, but when 'the man of the house' calls up, that's something else; right away there's respect, he's treated differently. That made me angry."

With the pressure and publicity mounting, things finally started moving more quickly. In July Audi announced that it would make still another repair to prevent sudden acceleration accidents—again, based on the company's assumption that the accidents were caused by driver error. This time the manufacturer offered to install a "shift-lock," a mechanism to prevent a driver from shifting out of "park" unless the brake pedal was firmly depressed. The company's action didn't appease Alice and Marion, who pointed out that almost invariably, the people who had experienced sudden acceleration accidents had been braking when their cars shot out of control.

In September, NHTSA finally upgraded its Audi investigation into a top-level investigation. And in November the Audi defect was the subject of an expose on national television, with a focus on the victims' network. Alice and Marion hoped that the national attention would finally bring effective action, but the result was hardly what they expected: In December, the federal government did request Audi to recall the car; the manufacturer's response was to agree to recall the automobile in order to install the same shift-lock device it had begun installing in cars months earlier. Meanwhile, the device wasn't working; even before Audi announced its latest recall, the women had heard of several sudden acceleration accidents involving cars in which the safety device had been installed. Reports of two more accidents came in within days of Audi's announcement. But Alice and Marion didn't give up. Instead, they started planning press conferences and other follow-up to show how inappropriate Audi and NHTSA's solution was.

"I'm an entirely different person now," says Alice. "This has improved my self-confidence—and I know that if you stand steadfast, you can accomplish something. I feel that I'll never let anyone take advantage of me again." She and Marion are considering starting an organization of their own as soon as the Audi issue is behind them—possibly a clearinghouse of information for other accident victims who have gotten nowhere in their dealings with manufacturers. "I never imagined I'd get involved this way—now I can't imagine going back to the way I was," Marion says. "When I started helping my husband with his dry cleaning business, I always knew it would be a temporary thing—that I'd go on to something else. I didn't know what it would be. Now I think I know, since we've gotten so much experience with this issue. I can do so many things that I never thought I could do—and it's a good feeling doing something I believe in."

Justice
and
Peace

"Good Noise"

Cora Tucker

"She was always making noise at school. We knew she'd grow up noisy. But it's good noise. When Cora talks, she knows what she's talking about."

Cora Tucker's house is so close to the railroad tracks that at night when trains thunder by, the beds shake. The house and furniture are modest, and in the kitchen there's a lingering smell of the lard Cora cooks with. There are traces of Virginia red clay on the kitchen floor, and piled up on the bedroom floor are cardboard boxes overflowing with newspaper clippings and other papers.

Cora admits she doesn't like housekeeping anymore. The plaques and photographs hanging in the kitchen and living room attest to what she does enjoy; alongside religious pictures and photos of her children and grandchildren, there are several citizenship awards, certificates acknowledging her work in civil rights, and photos of her—a pretty, smiling black woman—with various politicians. One framed picture in the kitchen was handmade for Cora by some of the inmates in a nearby prison, whom Cora has visited and helped. In it, Old English letters made of foil spell out, "God grant me the serenity to accept the things I cannot change, the courage to change the things I can, and wisdom to know the difference." Cora has plenty of all three virtues, although "serene" probably isn't the first adjective a stranger would pin on her. But then, there isn't much that Cora would say she can't change, either.

Cora Tucker is something of an institution in Halifax County, Virginia, a rural county bordering North Carolina. In more than a dozen years, she has missed only a handful of the county board of supervisors' monthly meetings. Her name appears in the letters columns of the two daily newspapers several times a week—either signed onto her own letter or, almost as often, vilified in someone else's. She seems to know and be known by every black person on the street, in the post offices, and in stores and restaurants. And she is known by white and black people alike as having taken on many of the local, white-controlled institutions. Her main concern is simply fighting for the underdog, which she does in many ways—from social work-like visits to the elderly and invalids, to legal fights against racial discrimination, registering people to vote, and lobbying on issues like health care and the environment.

Cora was born in 1941 ten miles from where she lives now, near the Halifax county seat, in the small town of South Boston. Her father was a school teacher and later a railway porter. He died when Cora was three, and her mother and the nine children became sharecroppers on white men's farms. It was as a sharecropper, Cora says, that she learned how to do community organizing. She started by trying to help other sharecroppers to get things like better heating and food stamps. "I didn't call it 'organizing,' then," she says. "I just called it 'being concerned.' When you do sharecropping, you move around a lot. So I got to know everybody in the county, and to know what people's problems were.

"'Sharecropping is the worst form of drudgery; it's slavery really. You work on a man's farm, supposedly for half the profit on the crops you grow. That's what the contract says. But you pay for all the stuff that goes into the crop—seeds, fertilizer, and all. You get free housing, but most sharecroppers' housing is dilapidated and cold. It isn't insulated—it's just shacks, really. Sharecroppers are poor. I know of a family of twelve who grew fifteen acres of tobacco, and at the end of the year, they had earned just fifty dollars. And I know sharecroppers who needed food and applied for food stamps, but couldn't get them because they supposedly made too much money; the boss went to the food stamp office, and said they made such and such, so they couldn't qualify."

Cora went to work very young, planting and plowing with the others in the family. Her mother taught her to cook when she was six; Cora remembers having to stand on a crate to reach the kitchen counter. She was a curious and intelligent child who loved school and was unhappy when she had to stay out of school to clean house for the white woman on the farm where they lived.

Cora always adored her mother. Bertha Plenty Moesley was a "chief stringer"—a step in tobacco processing that involves picking the green tobacco leaves from the plants one at a time, and stringing them together three leaves to a stick, so that they can be hung to dry and cure. "My mama worked hard," Cora says. "She would plow and do all the things the men did. She was independent; she raised her children alone for eighteen years. When I was little, I felt so bad that she had to work that hard just so we could survive. There was welfare out there—all kinds of help, if only somebody had told her how to go about getting it. She had very little education, and didn't know to go down to the welfare office for help. As I got older, I was upset by that and made up my mind, when I was about eight or nine years old, that if I ever got grown, I'd make sure that everybody knew how to get everything there was to get. And I really meant it. I learned early how to get things done, and I learned it would take initiative to get what I wanted."

By the time Cora learned about welfare, her mother wouldn't take advantage of it. She was proud, and she told the children to have self-respect. "We didn't have anything else," Cora's mother says. "The kids had only themselves to be proud of." Cora took the advice to heart. There's a story she tells about growing up that has found a permanent place in community-organizing lore. In her high school, which was segregated at the time (Halifax County schools didn't integrate until 1969, under court order), Cora entered an essay contest on the topic of "what America means to me." She was taken by surprise when her bitter essay about growing up black in the South won a statewide award. But on awards night she was in for another surprise. The winners were to have their essays read, and then shake hands with the Virginia governor. Cora's mother was in the audience beaming, along with Cora's friends and teachers. But when her essay was read, Cora didn't recognize it—it had been rewritten, and the less critical sentiments weren't hers at all. She refused to greet the governor. "I disappointed everyone—my mother even cried."

The only person who supported her that night, she says, was a high school literature teacher, whom she credits as an important influence on her. "He spent a lot of time with me, encouraging me. Every time an issue came up that I felt strongly about, he'd have me write about it—letters to the editor that never got printed. He told me, 'Nobody can make you a second class citizen but you. You should be involved in what's going on around you.'"

Instead, at seventeen she dropped out of high school to get married. As she describes it, the next several years were consumed with housekeeping and having children—six of them in rapid succession. She and her husband adopted a seventh. At first, Cora says, she threw herself enthusiastically into her new role. "I just wanted to be married. My father-in-law used to tease me about making myself so busy just being married. He'd say, 'You ain't going to keep this up for long.' But I'd say yes I would. Every morning, I put clean sheets on our beds—washed and ironed them. I ironed every diaper. I read all the housekeeping magazines; my house was immaculate. But I was beginning to find myself so bored, even then. My husband was farming then, sharecropping, and he'd get up early; I'd get up too, and feed him and the kids, and then do the cleaning. But when you clean every day, there just isn't that much to do, so I'd be finished by ten in the morning! I joined a book club, so that I would get a book every month—but I would get bored in between. I would read the book in two days—I tried to savor it, but I couldn't make it last any longer. Then, when the kids started growing up and going to school, that would occupy me a little more. I'd feed them, then take them to school, and come back and clean and then start making lunch. But just as soon as my baby started school, I went out and got a job."

Halifax County has several textile and garment factories, and Cora went to work as a seamstress for one of the largest, a knit sportswear manufacturer. It was a fairly new operation, and the mostly women employees were expected to do everything, from lifting fabric bolts weighing forty or fifty pounds each, to sitting at sewing machines for eight hour stretches. There was no union; the county boasts in promotional material that less than 5 percent of the county's workforce is unionized. "Every time I used to talk to the girls there, my boss thought I was trying to get a union started. And I sure thought there *should* be a union; there were lots of health hazards, and people were always getting hurt. People got back injuries, two people even had heart attacks in the factory, because of the working conditions. I once got a woman to come down from Baltimore to talk about forming a union, but people got frightened because the bosses warned us that if there was any union activity, we'd lose our jobs."

Cora worked at the factory for seven years. The first thing she did with the money she was earning was to buy land for a house. "We had lived in places where we were so cold," she says. "We'd have no windows, and no wood. My dream was always to grow up and build me a house—my own house, out of brick. My husband never really wanted one; he was just as happy moving around. But after I had the babies and went to work at the factory, I told him I was going to build me a house. So the first year I worked, I saved a thousand dollars. The next year I saved another thousand, and then borrowed some from the company, to buy some land. Then I started saving again, for the house. But when I went to the FHA, they said I couldn't get a house without my husband's permission. At first, he said he wasn't going to have anything to do with it, so I said I'd buy a trailer instead. When he found out, he figured I might just as well put the money into a house, so he signed the papers. We built the house; it was the first time any of us had been inside a new house. I was crazy about it; we could sit

down and say exactly where we wanted things. And while I was working, I bought every stick of furniture in it."

In 1976 Cora hurt her back and had to leave her job. Over the next
few years she underwent surgery several times—first for her back, and
then for cancer (for which she has had to have periodic treatments
ever since). In the meantime, she had become active in the community. In the 1960s, she had participated in organizations like the National Association for the Advancement of Colored People, and
another group called the Assemblies, but they moved too slowly for
her tastes. ("They weren't really interested in taking on the power
structure," she complains.) She had also organized her own letter-
writing campaign in support of the federal Voting Rights Act to make it
easier for blacks to vote. She had gone around to local churches,
speaking to people and encouraging them to write to their representatives in Washington. She also took advantage of knowing women who
ran beauty parlors—she provided the paper and pens, so that women
could write letters while they sat under the hair dryers. "People
would say to me, 'What good will it do?' But I think politicians have to
be responsive if enough pressure can be brought to bear on them. You
can complain, I can complain, but that's just two people. A politician
needs to get piles of letters saying vote for this bill, because if you
don't, you won't be in office much longer!" Cora was responsible for
generating about five hundred letters supporting the voting law.

She takes voting very seriously. In 1977, she campaigned for a pop-
ulist candidate for Virginia governor. She was undergoing cancer treatments at the time, but they made her tired, so she stopped the
treatments in order to register people to vote. She had taught herself
to drive, and personally rode around the county from house to house,
filling her car with everyone there who was of voting age, driving
them to the court house to register, and then home again. She's credited with having registered over one thousand people this way, and on
election day, she personally drove many of them to the polling place.

While Cora was growing up, her mother's house was always filled
with people—besides her own family, several cousins lived with them,
and aunts and uncles who had moved up north and came back to visit
would stay with Cora's mother. Cora's own house was the same way—
always filled with neighborhood teenagers, white and black. Cora became a confidante for the young people, and she encouraged them to
read about black history, and to be concerned about the community.
One of the things that upset the teenagers was the fate of a county
recreation center. Halifax had no recreation facilities, and the county

had applied for money from the federal Department of Housing and Urban Development (HUD) to build a center. When HUD awarded the county $500,000, however, the county turned it down because, as Cora puts it, there were "too many strings attached"—meaning it would have to be integrated. At home because of her back trouble and cancer, Cora took it on herself to help steer the teenagers' anger toward research into community problems. "When I heard about the recreation center, I went to the county board meeting and raised hell," she says. "But they went ahead and did what they wanted anyway. What I realized then was that if I had had all those kids come with me to the meeting, there would have been some changes. You need warm bodies—persons present and accounted for—if you want to get things done."

In 1975, Cora founded her own organization, Citizens for a Better America. CBA's first project was a study of black spending and employment patterns in the county. The study was based on a survey of three hundred people; it took two years to complete, with Cora's teenage friends doing much of the legwork. The findings painted a clear picture of inequality. Blacks made up nearly half the county population, and according to the survey, spent a disproportionate share of their salaries on food, cars, and furniture. But, as the study pointed out, there were very few black employees at the grocery stores where the money was spent, not a single black salesperson in the furniture stores, and no black salesperson at the auto dealerships. Blacks weren't represented at all on newspaper or radio station staffs.

Cora saw to it that the survey results were published in the local newspaper. The next step was to act on the results. The survey had uncovered problems with hiring practices and promotions of blacks in the school system, so Cora complained to the school board. After waiting in vain for the board to respond, CBA filed a complaint with what was then the federal Department of Health, Education, and Welfare. An HEW investigation confirmed the problems, and the agency threatened to cut off federal education funds to the county if the discrimination wasn't corrected. The county promised that the next principals it hired would be black.

CBA then took on other aspects of the county government. The survey had found that of all the county employees, only 7 percent were black—chiefly custodial workers or workers hired with federal Comprehensive Employment Training Administration (CETA) funds. Only one black person in the county government made over $20,000 a year. When the county refused to negotiate with Cora's organization about their hiring practices, CBA filed a complaint with the federal revenue sharing program. A Virginia state senator was successful in getting a federal investigation into the complaint stalled, but Cora went over his head, to the congressional Black Caucus and Maryland's black congressman, Parren Mitchell. Mitchell contacted Senator Edward Kennedy's office, which pressed to have the investigation completed. The findings confirmed CBA's, and the county was told to improve its hiring practices or stand to lose federal revenues.

CBA also initiated a boycott of local businesses that didn't hire minorities—Cora avoided the term "boycott," and instead called the action the "Spend Your Money Wisely Campaign." Leaflets were distributed listing the stores that hired black employees, and urging people, "Where Blacks are not HIRED, Blacks should not buy!"

Cora was developing a reputation. She started having frequent contact with the congressional Black Caucus, and would be called occasionally to testify in Washington on welfare issues. "They don't usually get people like me to testify; they get all these 'experts' instead. But every once in a while, it's good for them to hear from someone who isn't a professional, whose English isn't good, and who talks from a grassroots level."

It wasn't just in Washington that her reputation was growing, but back home, too. "I have a lot of enemies," she says. "There are derogatory things in the papers about me all the time. And the county government doesn't like me, because I keep going to all those board meetings and raising hell about what they do. When I go sometimes, they say, 'Yes, what do you want now, Ms. Tucker?' But I don't care what they think—I just tell them what I want. So a lot of the white power structure don't really like me. They think I'm a troublemaker, but I'm not really. I just believe what I believe in. Then there are black people too, who think that I want too much too soon. But when you think about it, black people have been in America 360-some years, so when is the time ever going to be right? The time doesn't *get* right; you make it right. So I'm not offended by what anybody says about me."

Sometimes the problem isn't just what people say; it's what they do. Cora has had many experiences with harassment. At first it was phone calls, from people threatening to burn her house down or telling her to "go back to Africa." Once she wrote a letter to the editor saying, "This is an open letter to all the people who call me and ask, what do you niggers want now? and hang up before I can tell them. . .

Blacks and poor people want to share in the economic progress of Halifax County, and when we get our children educated and motivated we would like them to come back to Halifax County and do something other than push mops and brooms. And a few of us would like our grandchildren to grow up near us, and if our children decide to make their home elsewhere it will be due to choice and not an economic necessity."

The harassment has taken other forms as well. Cora was followed and run off the highway one night, and had all four tires slashed one day when her car was parked in town. Once she was in the post office and a man recognized her, walked over, and spit on her; another time a car with out-of-state license plates pulled up next to her car as if to ask directions, and the man spat into her face. She came home from a meeting one night to find that someone had broken into her home and drenched her bed with gasoline. But Cora views the abuses with amazing equanimity: "If you stop doing things because somebody says something bad about you or does something to you," she says, "then you'll never get *anything* done."

And she wasn't making only enemies; she was also gaining a following. One woman, who now works in the local legal aid office where Cora stops in frequently to get answers to legal questions, tells how she first met Cora. The woman had been born in Halifax, but had moved to New Jersey when she was a young girl. The civil rights movement progressed, and when the woman was finished with school, she moved back to Virginia, thinking that things there would be much better than they *had* been for blacks. But she found that any progress had been superficial only. When she started looking for work, she discovered there there were no blacks in responsible positions. She wore her hair in an Afro, and in hindsight thinks that it cost her jobs: At one point, it seemed she would be offered a position with the county, but when the man who was to be her boss saw her, he didn't give her the job. Another prospective employer turned her down with the flat statement that he didn't want any union people around.

She became disillusioned, and was shocked at the complacency around her. About that time, she saw Cora Tucker's name in the paper. She was impressed, and started asking around about Cora. Not too long afterwards, she went to a community action program meeting, and noticed that Cora was scheduled to speak. "I was excited. I thought, finally, I'm going to meet a black person who's alive!" But she was initially disappointed. "I had pictured her as a towering woman—a fiery, eloquent speaker, like Barbara Jordan. Instead, there she was, short, and not that articulate."

But she quickly got drawn to Cora's strengths. "Cora wouldn't be happy at home, doing housekeeping," she says. "She's just not cut out for that. She's cut out for doing exactly what she's doing—getting out and raising hell about issues that affect people. She keeps pushing. When I get burned, I back off. But when Cora gets burned, she just blows out the fire and goes on."

Even people who don't like Cora give her credit: "I'm not a Cora Tucker fan," says one South Boston resident. "But I admit that she might just be the most informed person on political issues in this county." People credit Cora with having stamina and with inspiring others. An old friend of hers who runs a corner grocery says, "She keeps people fired up; she won't let us get lazy. It's because of her that I even watch the news!" One woman who was in school with Cora and now works for the county government says, "She was always making noise at school. We knew she'd grow up noisy. But it's *good* noise. When Cora talks, she knows what she's talking about."

And although Cora thinks she'll never be much of a public speaker, others disagree. One man who has worked with Cora for several years described a dinner ceremony sponsored by a human rights coalition in Richmond. "They had asked Cora to come and be a featured speaker. The woman who spoke before her gave this very polished speech. And then Cora got up, and gave her very unpolished speech. But it was moving to everyone in the room, because it was so much from the heart. It was the contrast of day and night between her and the previous speaker. What she had to say was so honest and down to earth, that people were very touched by it. And that's just the way she is."

Cora is very religious. "I believe in God, and in the providence of prayer. I go to church regularly." The churches in her area are still segregated; she attends the Crystal Hill Baptist Church, which, she points out with a chuckle, is brick-colored, while the white congregation down the road painted their brick church white. In an essay called "Halifax County and Blacks," under a subtitle "Things Blacks Must Do To Succeed," Cora once wrote, "First, blacks must go to church. The church is the backbone of black progress." Every summer for several years Cora has organized a "Citizenship Day of Prayer" on the lawn of the county courthouse in South Boston, which attracts hundreds of people who probably wouldn't gather if the event were called a rally. At the event a list of grievances is always read off— including complaints about such things as how people are treated by the welfare system, unfair employment practices, or disproportionate suspensions of black pupils in the schools.

Problems like that—and what to do about them—are raised regularly at Citizens for a Better America meetings, held the fourth Friday of each month at a local funeral home. CBA has several hundred members, and with help from friends, Cora publishes a monthly one-page newsletter, which she decorates with American flag stickers and short religious sayings. The newsletter is a hodgepodge of useful information, including notices of food stamp law changes, regular updates on what the Virginia General Assembly is considering, board of supervisors' actions, community news, and news about other subjects that Cora is currently concerned with. One issue might have an essay on education, something on federal budget cutbacks and poor people, and a paragraph on the dangers of uranium mining. In 1986, when the federal government was considering southern Virginia, including part of Halifax County, as a possible site for a high-level nuclear waste dump, Cora and CBA fought back, using a section of the federal law requiring that the siting consideration take Indians and other minorities into account. Among other things, CBA found that blacks owned more farmland in Halifax County than in any other county in the country, and that historically, the first black-owned businesses and land in the country were on the site that would be affected by the nuclear waste dump.

Cora learns facts quickly; she can attend a meeting on the problems of family farmers one day, and the next, go to another meeting and be able to reel off facts and figures about farm foreclosures, the cost of fertilizers, trends in agribusiness, and the harmful effect of various pesticides. She reads constantly—newspapers, books, anything on an issue that interests her. "I save newspaper clippings—especially statements from politicians. That way, five years from now when they say, 'I'm definitely against that,' I can go back and say, 'But on such and such a date, you said *this*.'"

Cora stays extremely busy. Several years ago, she went back and got her graduate equivalency diploma, and took some courses at the community college. She thought she might want her degree: "I used to think I wanted to be a social worker. But I changed my mind, because you can't do as much inside the system as you can on the outside. There are so many people who become social workers, and then sit there with their hands tied. What people really need is somebody on the outside who's going to go and raise hell for them about laws and regulations."

Besides CBA gatherings, meetings of the county board of supervisors, and her usual rounds to the legal aid office and the county office building, Cora still visits elderly people, helps women without cars to do their shopping, reads and explains people's mail about food stamps and social security to them, and answers frequent letters. She takes every letter seriously. One, for instance, addressed simply to "Cora Tucker, Halifax, Virginia," read, "Dear Mrs. Tucker, Please don't let the county send us to be experimented on. We heard that they are going to take people on welfare to be experimented on." Cora remembered that there had been separate articles in the newspaper recently, on the "workfare" program to employ welfare recipients, and on a county decision to allow dogs from the animal pound to be used for medical experiments. Cora concluded that the person who wrote the letter had gotten the two issues confused—but she wasn't satisfied until she had called the county administrator and had gotten him to pledge to do a better job of explaining the issues publicly.

Cora's work goes far beyond Halifax. CBA itself has chapters in several other places, including one started in Baltimore by one of Cora's sisters. In addition, when a new coalition group, Virginia Action, was started in the state in 1980, Cora was on the founding committee and was elected its first president. She also became active on the board of its national affiliate, Citizen Action. And in 1981, on top of everything else she was doing, this woman who as a girl had refused to shake the governor's hand was talked into running as a write-in protest candidate for governor by several black groups. She didn't get many votes, but her campaign was covered in the press, and she thinks that she raised issues about black people's concerns that otherwise would have been ignored.

Cora hasn't received much support in her work from her family, except from her mother. She and her husband are estranged, and her children haven't taken an active interest in Cora's work. Cora visits her mother often, in an old house several miles away that has woodburning stoves for heat, religious pictures in the downstairs room, and, hanging in the stairway, a plastic placemat depicting Martin Luther King's tomb. Cora's mother is clearly proud of her; she emphasizes what a smart girl Cora was, and is, and how courageous.

Others agree. As a man who works with Cora at Virginia Action puts it, "All of the issues Cora has taken on—like voting rights and employment discrimination—had been problems in Halifax County for decades. But nobody was willing to fight. And the reason was that it's very, very hard to be somebody going against the mainstream in a small rural community. It's a hell of a lot easier to play the role of the gadfly when you live in an urban environment, where you have your own community of friends, and you don't have to worry about the world. In a small rural community, your community *is* your world.

And it's hard to fight the people you have to face every single day. Cora's able to do it because she's got guts. There's just nothing else to it but courage. In a small community those people writing nasty letters to the editor about you are people you're going to run into at the grocery, or whose kids go to school with yours. In addition, being black in a southern rural community, and being a woman, make it that much harder. She hasn't even had the active support of a large part of the black community—they feel threatened by her; she's stolen a lot of their fire. And she's always fighting back as opposed to the blacks who always cooperate with the white power structure. She just reached a point where she decided that slow-moving efforts weren't enough for the things that needed doing—things that were clear in her mind. She recognized the dangers that would be involved, but went ahead because she knew she was right."

"Emboldened"

Greenham Common Women

9

"There have been actions by women all over the world in support of what the protests at Greenham represent. Women have taken actions, some quite strenuous, who had never taken any action of this kind in their lives. They're emboldened in a way they wouldn't have dreamt of before."

*I*n late 1979, in what amounted to a major new escalation of the nuclear arms race, NATO announced the decision to deploy a new arsenal of several hundred U.S. nuclear missiles in Western Europe. The first of these, ninety-six ground launched cruise missiles, were to be installed in 1983 at the U.S. air base at Greenham Common, near Newbury, England, about sixty miles west of London.

In September 1981, forty British women walked 120 miles from Wales to Greenham Common to protest and call public attention to the preparations that were under way at the base to receive the missiles. The public didn't get a chance to hear about the women's action, though, since the media ignored the march. When they arrived at the base, the women decided to protest the lack of attention to the issue by staying at the base, and the Greenham Common women's "peace camp" evolved as an ongoing vigil outside the base's gates. The original goal of the protest was the modest one of stirring up a public debate on the new nuclear weapons, but as more and more women joined the effort and the protest started receiving international attention, the goal became to block the deployment of the missiles at Greenham.

That round was lost when the first cruise missiles arrived at the base in November 1983, but women stayed on, maintaining the camp as a permanent protest against those missiles and all nuclear weapons. The numbers of women who actually camp out at the base at a given time has varied, and the physical character of the camp has changed. A relatively comfortable cluster of tents and wood-and-plastic shelters gave way to more temporary, portable shelters when officials started regularly "evicting" the women from the government land outside the gates of the base. Still the protest has continued—day and night, through all seasons, in sun or rain (mostly rain, in that part of England).

The women's protest at Greenham Common inspired many other peace camps across Europe and in the United States, and infused new vitality into the peace movement. In addition to the women living at the base itself, a large network emerged, made up of women across Britain who were motivated to peace activism. Several large actions, involving up to fifty thousand women at a time, have been held at the base every year since the camp was started.

For many of the women, involvement in the issue has led to major changes in their lives. Women who had never considered breaking the law have been arrested and jailed for civil disobedience. Some of the women's marriages have broken apart because of the intensity of their involvement. Some have quit their professions to work full time as peace activists.

What has made this movement special is the direct and emotional nature of the commitment of the women involved. The term "Greenham women" doesn't refer to an organization with a structure, members, and leaders—and doesn't refer only to those women living at the camp. Instead it has come to be synonymous with a contagious, personal form of commitment—an intense determination to do whatever is possible as individuals to bring about change in military and nuclear policy, a policy area where people usually feel particularly powerless.

Here are four women's accounts, in their own words, of their involvement in Greenham Common. The statements of Simone Wilkinson, Susan Lamb, and Helen Johns are from interviews in 1983, before the missiles arrived. Deborah Law's statement is from an interview in 1985.

Simone Wilkinson:

I had always been aware of nuclear weapons, and had been very afraid of war since I was child, because my family suffered so much during World War II. One thing that brought the nuclear issue home to me happened when I was eight months pregnant with my second child. I was at a party in London, and I overheard a Japanese woman there say that her uncle had been a survivor at Hiroshima. And I blurted out—rather glibly I'm afraid—"Oh, that must have been an awful experience!" I suppose because I was so very pregnant, she turned to me and said, "Yes it was. And even today in Hiroshima, when a woman becomes pregnant, no one congratulates her. They just wait silently for nine months, because so many children are still being born deformed."

That really struck a chord, and I began reading about nuclear issues. And although I still didn't get involved in the peace movement, everything I heard about the arms race touched off something in my consciousness—it was like the steady dripping of water somewhere. What finally gave me the push I needed was when the government engaged in a civil defense campaign, and started publicizing how people could protect themselves in the event of nuclear war. The government's plan involved tearing doors in your house off their hinges, leaning four of them together into a kind of shelter, and crawling in there, with your family and enough rations for a fortnight. I knew—everyone knew—that that couldn't begin to protect you.

The whole thing sent me into a panic, and I worked myself into a state of total despair. I would have conversations about nuclear war with friends, and if they didn't feel as strongly about it as I did—if they brushed it off—I would start in raving at them. I would listen to the radio first thing in the morning, and hear that the Russians had said such and such, and the Americans such and such, and I would call out to my husband, "Christ, listen to them—they're going to have a nuclear war!" This went on for weeks, with some periods of relative calm, but generally I wasn't just upset, I was frantic! Finally my husband told me if I felt that strongly about it then I'd better do something, because I wasn't doing myself or the children any good going on this way.

So I joined the local peace movement. Right away it struck me that for many of those people, pacifism was simply the way they were brought up; they had joined the peace movement automatically, the way they'd join any other club. We had the usual monthly meetings and planned the usual marches, but all that seemed incongruous to me when what was at stake was nuclear war. By this time, the Greenham Common peace camp had been under way for about two and a half weeks. A friend of mine was going up to visit it, and I decided to go along with her for the day.

I don't know what I expected—maybe a bunch of young hippies. But I was amazed when I got there; the first person I met was the epitome of respectability, a Welsh grandmother who had been part of the original march. The determination of the women was so straightforward—something I could plug into from the beginning. I was filled with emotion, because I thought, thank God, here are other people who have been grabbed by this the same way I have.

So naturally I began getting involved in the camp, and as I spent more time there, my outlook finally began to improve. I had joined the peace movement out of sheer, total despair. Every day I had gotten up and there was tremendous sadness inside me. Now I was witnessing the creativity of women. They were living on a piece of wasteland, and out of sticks and plastic they had built beautiful shelters. And what they were doing there was so clearcut and simple—just being there, a constant presence, talking to people about their concerns. That simplicity was the joy of Greenham, that and finding others who felt as intensely as I did, and who were dealing with their fear so directly, finding a way of coping with it, not by suppressing it but by facing it openly.

When I became involved in civil disobedience, it was a very big step for me, because I come from a very conservative background. I took an act of civil disobedience because I felt that there was nothing else I could do but put my body against the war machine with hundreds of others who were doing the same thing. And when I did it the first time, I really felt like I'd taken on the world. We blockaded the base, and I remember the next day feeling that we'd done it, that was the end of cruise. I realized very quickly that it wasn't, but it did give us a lot of courage to take actions like that.

Then in August 1982 a group of us entered the base illegally, and in November we were sent to prison for two weeks. It was a deliberate action, to bring the issue to court and before the public. Although afterwards there was a lot of talk about the brave and courageous Greenham women, I had been terrified. I had qualms about how my family would cope with my going to prison, and I was anxious about it for myself—it was such an unknown, this whole experience of going to prison. I never questioned that it was the right thing to do. As it was, the experience in many ways wasn't too bad, because we were all together. The worst part was after we were sentenced, when we were sent to cells below and were pushed into the back of a prison van, with separate compartments inside. That was the ultimate culture shock for me—finding myself in this box, touching the sides and the back, and my knees pushed up against the door. It was all made out of steel, and very cold. They left us there for two and a half hours, while they decided where they were taking us. I've never felt anything like it in my life.

There are people who say you've got to arm yourself with all the facts, that you have to know all the statistics and arguments before you can go out and talk about this. But that's numbing and intimidating, especially in an issue like this, when really all you need to know is that the policy is wrong. The first time I ever did a street campaign, I knew nothing—I didn't even know what a cruise missile was. But I was frantic about nuclear war. I had a petition for people to sign. I just went out there with it, but within the first five minutes I realized I didn't know what I'd say if people came up with arguments. And sure enough they did, and I didn't know how to dispute them. I got almost to the point of tears when this one man went on and on about you can't trust the Russians, and how did I know they wouldn't cheat on arms control—because in my gut I thought that what he was saying didn't make any sense, but I didn't know how to argue back. And I finally looked at him and took a deep breath and said, "I don't know the answer. All I know is that this weapon policy is wrong, and I'm not going to sit back and let it continue."

I can live with myself now because I know I'm being true to myself. If the world went up in explosion tomorrow, and we were all at the day of judgment, or the gates of St. Peter, or whatever, and he said, "Well, what about the fact that the world went up in a nuclear explosion?" I wouldn't be standing there saying, "Oh well, I've always thought it was terrible, but it had nothing to do with me." I would say I did everything—everything that I could. I can live with myself and die with myself because I have no doubts about what I'm doing.

Susan Lamb:

I think I always realized that I should be doing something about this issue of nuclear weapons, but it always came down to the question of what I could really do. I just felt there was nothing that I could actually do to change things. What ended up shaking me out of that helplessness was my child's fear. It was a contagious thing; I began to think about nuclear war in a new way, about the immenseness of it, the finality of it.

When my daughter was two, I took her on a day's outing to the London zoo, which involves catching the train, and riding across the country from Wales. Over the zoo is the flight path for Heathrow Airport, and an airplane passes over every few minutes all day long. The day turned into a nightmare, because with every airplane that passed over, my daughter became increasingly hysterical, saying, "They're going to bomb us, they're going to bomb us!" I tried to calm her down, and tell her they were simply taking people to other countries, on holiday. But by the end of the day, riding back on the train, I was in a cold sweat myself because I'd begun to realize as the afternoon went by that that's just about how far away we are from a nuclear war. The warning I would probably receive would be minutes, if I were lucky. On the train I started thinking, this train is going 125 miles an hour—would that be fast enough to escape a blast from an atomic explosion? And I began to think of my whole life in those terms.

A couple months later I went to a public meeting about nuclear weapons policy, and someone there was talking about people having to taking personal responsibility for it. And thinking about it in those terms, I decided that however little I had to contribute I had to do something, so I joined in the local peace group, and started going to meetings and joining in campaigns, like petitioning for a nuclear free zone. I knew about the women's march to Greenham, and I thought it was a grand idea, but my family had made holiday arrangements for then, and I thought it would be too difficult to march all the way with two little children anyway. Then about six weeks later we heard that the women were still there at Greenham, living there day in and day out, but the public didn't know about it because the word wasn't getting out.

We realized that obviously we in the peace movement weren't being very effective; it was all very well to go to meetings and talk to people and allay our fears that way, but we simply weren't getting across to other people. So a group of my friends and I decided that we would take responsibility for letting the people in our town know about the missiles and the Greenham Common peace camp; and we mimicked what they were doing at Greenham by camping out in the town square for a week. We didn't like doing it. I was worried sick about doing it, really—worried about what people would say, wondering if I'd rather be ignored, or have people point at me and say I was crazy. It was our neighbors we'd be standing up in front of, exposed that way. In a way, it would have been easier to go away and do something like that somewhere else, because then if it went completely wrong and we made utter fools of ourselves, at least it wouldn't be in front of people we lived with, and would go on living with.

It was about seven o'clock on a Wednesday morning when we arrived at the town square. By eleven o'clock, my whole attitude toward life had changed. I realized that I had power that I never thought I had. Because while we were there, we had all kinds of people coming up to us and blessing us, and offering us things to keep us warm, and pensioners bringing us cups of soup out of their houses, as a gesture of thanks for doing what we were doing.

The same sort of thing happened when we went to prison for entering the base. We were the players, the court was the stage, and we created the audience, through things as simple as a chain letter telling people what was going on. So when we went to prison there was an uproar in our country from people who thought it was wrong to send women to prison for following their consciences. After we got out, we held a demonstration at Greenham Common—thirty thousand women came, and they held hands with one another, surrounding the base, and gave their commitment to work together and not allow this evil to continue. The next day, four thousand women prepared themselves to be arrested if necessary, and sat down and blockaded the base. Many women were treated harshly. But each of those women had made a commitment. When they were moved, they brushed themselves off, brushed off their friends, and walked back and sat there again.

When the women came to that action, each of them brought with her a token representing why she was there, and pinned it to the fence surrounding the base. It was one of the most moving experiences I ever had in my life, to walk around the perimeter of that fence, and see all the children's booties, the poems, the baby gloves, and all sorts of small mementos of people's lives. One thing that had me in floods of tears was a photograph of a child, and underneath it, the words, "My child died last September. I have put her photograph here in the hope that other mothers do not have to lose their children."

My involvement with Greenham hasn't been easy. At one point, it looked as if I stood to lose everything that had motivated me to join the peace movement. I had always thought of marriage as the base for two people to move out from and come back to for support. But when it came down to it, it was that way for my husband, while I was the home base. When I started doing this work, I wanted to be able to look at the marriage as a base in the same way. We started having big arguments about it, and finally he basically said to me, "Look, it's me or the peace movement." I was forced to think, was it worth continuing what I was doing, and risk losing the very thing—my family—that had pushed me to do it? And I said to him, "If I sit here and don't do anything, I'll lose all respect for myself and for you, and we'll lose what we have anyway." So I continued, with his support. There's no point in making that kind of compromise, or being expedient. You have to be true to yourself.

Women have initiated this action because women are the ones excluded from the meaningless bureaucracy of peace groups. We're the ones who can't cope with it, who totally reject it, and want to walk away and leave the men to carry on with their utterly mundane and irrelevant discussions. That's what's so beautiful about Greenham: You go there, and you experience it and you walk away feeling very strong willed because you know that no matter what happens, women there are doing what they believe in. Someone is standing up for something good.

Greenham works because of the sheer physical presence of the women, not just at the base, but going around talking at meetings, talking to the press, going to union meetings, even parties—trying to show that it's possible to act in a positive way on this issue.

I've totally changed since I've been involved. I was very insecure, and had very low self-esteem. Now I know what I can do. I know that I have a right to speak my mind as much as any other person.

Helen John:

A few years ago, my life was completely average—I was at home, raising a family, not political at all. I voted at general election time, and left others to make the decisions the rest of the time. That's all changed now, because of cruise missiles. I've taken the other view now—that I can't leave other people with the responsibility of ridding us of these missiles; I'm now doing it for myself. Probably all of us should have been doing it a great deal earlier.

I'm a mother, and have five children, and a very considerable drive for me has been the fact that I want those children to grow up and have normal, happy, healthy lives—the way one would reasonably expect one's children to live. The terrifying experience of watching the construction of the silos to put the cruise missiles in has made me well aware that this is not likely to happen, unless we get policies changed very fast. I didn't really consider myself a pacifist before this, though I've never had the slightest idea to kill anybody, and I chose to work as a nurse and midwife, so I have a very strong inclination to keep people alive.

Our tactics are to show people what we believe, and show them their own power. For instance, when we go into the base, the police there can't really believe that we're monsters, or communist subversives, or whatever. They have to understand that we're frightened for our lives and our children's lives. The men who are daily preparing weapons of mass destruction—I think they close their minds to that reality, but it doesn't work forever. In the end those men will realize it's as much their lives as anyone else's that are being affected. We're there to remind them. And I think we've been enormously successful in helping women act in a very positive, determined manner. There have been actions by women all over the world in support of what the protests at Greenham represent. In many cases, large numbers of women have taken actions, some quite strenuous, who had never taken any action of this kind in their lives. I think that's because of the Greenham example; they identify with it because they see it as being effective; they're emboldened in a way they wouldn't have dreamt of before.

I've always got on very easily with people. I like people, like to be with them, and I quite enjoy myself doing this, and I think that rubs off on people. My whole life is taken up with this work now. I'm really a very lazy person by nature—I rarely if ever do anything I don't really want to do, or haven't got my heart in. This I want to do, and my whole heart's in it. Every one of us has to be responsible for what happens in our own name, and our governments are behaving in this manner now because so many people are not standing up and protesting. If more individuals would say simply they don't want nuclear weapons, it could be stopped very quickly, because you can't force people to have what they don't want. Once you make that decision, make up your own mind that you will no longer cooperate with this insanity, you are then in the position to influence so many other people that the whole thing is slowly boiling and growing. These protests are growing because it's a very enjoyable way of life—it's choosing life as opposed to death, that's the essential thing.

Deborah Law:

When I was about twelve, I started having nightmares about nuclear war. I was very keen for my parents to build a shelter; I couldn't think of a better way for them to spend their money. This was because from the moment I had known about nuclear weapons, I was terrified of them. I remember incredible tension one evening—it must have been during the Cuban missile crisis—my mother was very frightened. She took me down into the basement to a closet we never used and told me that if anything ever happened and she or my father weren't there, I was to get inside it. She was obviously very agitated, but tried not to convey it. And so I started having my nightmares.

Later I met a friend named Alice, and we found that we both were frightened of nuclear war. We had loads and loads of conversations about it, every time we met up. We were conscious that our men friends didn't share the same anxieties, and we couldn't understand why. I had never been part of a peace organization. I was wary of groups and organizations; I questioned the sense of identity one got through them, and I'd seen the infighting that goes on. Alice and I did go to one peace group meeting in an attempt to do something positive about our fears. But it was just horrible, really. They were making plans for some kind of sale or something, and none of it seemed right. After the meeting we said we'd go again, but we never did.

Then Alice read something about the Greenham peace camp, and went down to have a look at it. When she came back, she told me about a demonstration that was being planned. It was to be at the spring solstice, a celebration of life. So I went down for it. I didn't know much about the peace camp at all, except what Alice had told me—that some very ordinary women had gone to a place that was going to have nuclear weapons, and said they were going to stay there as long as necessary to keep them away. Up until then, I didn't know there *were* any nuclear weapons in England, and I was horrified. My picture of nuclear war hadn't included that; I had thought it was something between the United States and Russia.

When I got to the camp, there were lots of people milling around. In the course of the day I heard that some women were going to blockade the base for twenty-four hours; and that anyone who wanted to could join them. So I went and sat in the woods to think about what to do. I figured that if I believed in what these women were doing, and admitted that it should be done, then why should I be exempt from doing it myself? So I went to join the women in the tent who were preparing for the blockade; I got there late, just minutes before it began.

I was there for the twenty-four hours, and it totally changed things for me. I was high as a kite when I came back. I had this sense of power that comes from being able to express what I felt, and in the company of others doing the same thing. There was a wonderful spirit to it: Here were all these women, and we found that the only songs that we all knew in common were from "The Sound of Music." So there we were, at four o'clock in the morning, with this military base behind us, belting out anything we could remember from it. The symbol of what we were doing was so strong back then, that the soldiers wouldn't walk past us. They didn't know what to do; they hadn't yet had their training in how to act. We wouldn't have done anything, really; we wouldn't have bitten their ankles! But they didn't even try to get by. At one point there were even policemen doing an Irish jig with some of the women. They'd hung up their hats on a tree, and were dancing. But then the senior inspector came, and shot them away in a van. They had to come back five minutes later, shamefaced, to pick up their hats.

That blockade was the turning point for me. Afterwards, I read a description about the demonstration in a magazine, and was horrified at what it said, so I wrote a letter telling what it had really been like. It became important to me how the camp was portrayed in the media. Later I went down again, and found they needed help with some basic, indoor things like telephoning and keeping up an address list. I did that kind of work, and went down for demonstrations. It was quite a small network then, so that anytime something was planned, you were called and could just go down. I felt I didn't want to live there at the camp, but knew it was important that some women did, so I gave any support I could.

At that stage, I had no idea how many cruise missiles were planned for the base, and how many there were altogether. I had a notion that there might be a hundred of them altogether in the world. Very quickly I found out there were thousands of these weapons. But I still thought we could keep the cruise from coming—and I knew it was wrong not to try. I imagined the short space, the time right after a nuclear attack, and how I would feel if I hadn't done something. So it wasn't even necessarily a matter of believing that we could stop it from happening—it was a matter of whether I would contribute to it happening or not.

Things became very demoralizing around the time of the general election in 1983. People had the opportunity then to vote on cruise, but the way it ended up, that issue figured fifth or sixth in how people voted. *That's* when I thought that cruise was going to come, having watched that election. The camp itself was being ripped to pieces by the media. They'd gone through the praise phase, and were concentrating now on personal, sleazy stuff—criticizing the lifestyles of the women.

The cruise missiles arrived at the end of November. I saw one of the huge carriers landing. It was awful, watching it happen, so I sat down in the middle of the road to block traffic. I hadn't planned to do that. It was a primitive gesture, but I had to do *something*. It was all very confusing then, because everything up to that point had been geared to stopping cruise from coming. The next step was, now that they were here, we'd stop them from going out on exercises on the convoys. We were all going around in circles at that stage, demoralized and exhausted, and trying to think of what to do next. When the convoys go out there's a huge military and police escort; the police cordon off the base, and the convoys leave at a terrific pace. So the strategy became tracking them down—and in those terms, the military has failed, since we can know where they are; there's a fantastic network for tracking them down across the country for however long they're out. But it's terrifying seeing this thing—this police state—happening. Unless you directly confront something like that, you don't know the face of what you're confronting. You don't get that same impression from police when you're going about your daily business; it's not the same as the image of men behind helmets. When I saw the convoy go out, it was at the spot—the very same spot—where the four policemen had been dancing that night.

We began our involvement by talking about our fears of nuclear war, and it was through that that we found the strength to take actions. Whenever we talked to others and to the press, we kept saying, "Yes, we're going to stop cruise." But we denied our own despair, over perhaps *not* stopping it. We'd be saying to ourselves and others, "We can stop it. We can stop it. We can stop it." All the while, we were witnessing this huge military machinery in action. But we had to keep saying we could stop it. It was sickening, unhealthy; we were isolated and despairing. Only we didn't talk about it.

Now lots of the women are talking about it, and having gone through that and come out again, there's another wave of determination. We may not "succeed," but unless you contribute to trying to make a more positive way of living together, then you're certain to fail. And it's difficult to see in what way life may be changing now. It may be that the effect of so many people not wishing this course *is* actually holding things back. Maybe it would be going much faster otherwise.

It's going to take a deep, fundamental change in how we live. I've come to think it's very important to focus on images that affirm life rather than visualize its destruction. The military permanently visualizes destruction and makes things that are capable of destruction. To counteract that, you've got to affirm life—that's the only way of putting it. It seems very important to believe in a future, and not get into a state of mind where you think everything is coming to an end. But you have to believe in a future and, at the same time, not wear blinders. It's difficult. I can't say anymore that to do what I'm doing is going to stop nuclear weapons, because now I know the scale of things. But I also think that in a long term view of humanity's development, this is an important time. It's a turning point; it can go in either direction. It seems important to be helping in the pull toward another way of living.

In late 1987, U.S. and Soviet leaders announced their agreement on a treaty eliminating intermediate-range nuclear weapons, includ-

ing the cruise missiles based at Greenham. Although the treaty covers just 4 percent of the world's nuclear arsenal, and there are many unanswered questions about how it will be implemented, it represents an important first step in nuclear arms reduction.

About the Author

Anne Witte Garland worked for seven years as staff writer and editor for consumer and environmental advocacy organizations in Washington, DC and New York. She now lives in New York City and is a freelance writer covering environmental, public health, consumer, and women's issues.

Ralph Nader, internationally known public interest activist, is director of the Center for Study of Responsive Law, which sponsored the research and writing of this book.

Frances T. Farenthold, lawyer, educator, and peace activist, is former president of Wells College, and current chair of the board of directors of the Institute for Policy Studies in Washington, DC.

The Feminist Press at The City University of New York offers alternatives in education and in literature. Founded in 1970, this nonprofit, tax-exempt educational and publishing organization works to eliminate sexual stereotypes in books and schools and to provide literature with a broad vision of human potential. The publishing program includes reprints of important works by women, feminist biographies of women, and nonsexist children's books. Curricular materials, bibliographies, directories, and a quarterly journal provide information and support for students and teachers of women's studies. In-service projects help to transform teaching methods and curricula. Through publications and projects, The Feminist Press contributes to the rediscovery of the history of women and the emergence of a more humane society.

NEW AND FORTHCOMING BOOKS

Carrie Chapman Catt: A Public Life, by Jacqueline Van Voris. $24.95 cloth.

Competition: A Feminist Taboo? edited by Valerie Miner and Helen E. Longino. Foreword by Nell Irvin Painter. $29.95 cloth, $12.95 paper.

Daughter of Earth, a novel by Agnes Smedley. Foreword by Alice Walker. Afterword by Nancy Hoffman. $8.95 paper.

Doctor Zay, a novel by Elizabeth Stuart Phelps. Afterword by Michael Sartisky. $8.95 paper.

Get Smart: A Woman's Guide to Equality on Campus, by S. Montana Katz and Veronica Vieland. $29.95 cloth, $9.95 paper.

Harem Years: The Memoirs of an Egyptian Feminist, 1879-1924, by Huda Shaarawi. Translated and edited by Margot Badran. $29.95 cloth, $9.95 paper.

Leaving Home, a novel by Elizabeth Janeway. New Foreword by the author. Afterword by Rachel M. Brownstein. $8.95 paper.

Library and Information Sources on Women: A Guide to Collections in the Greater New York Area, compiled by the Women's Resources Group of the Greater New York Metropolitan Area Chapter of the Association of College and Research Libraries and the Center for the Study of Women and Society of the Graduate School and University Center of The City University of New York. $12.95 paper.

Lone Voyagers: Academic Women in Coeducational Universities, 1869-1937, edited by Geraldine J. Clifford. $29.95 cloth, $12.95 paper.

My Mother Marries, a novel by Moa Martinson. Translated and introduced by Margaret S. Lacy. $8.95 paper.

Sultana's Dream and Selections from The Secluded Ones, by Rokeya Sakhawat Hossain. Edited and translated by Roushan Jahan. Afterword by Hanna Papanek. $16.95 cloth, $6.95 paper.

Turning the World Upside Down: The Anti-Slavery Convention of American Women Held in New York City, May 9-12, 1837. Introduction by Dorothy Sterling. $2.95 paper.

With Wings: An Anthology of Literature by and about Women with Disabilities, edited by Marsha Saxton and Florence Howe. $29.95 cloth, $12.95 paper.

Writing Red: An Anthology of American Women Writers, 1930-1940, edited by Charlotte Nekola and Paula Rabinowitz. Foreword by Toni Morrison. $29.95 cloth, $12.95 paper.

FICTION CLASSICS

Between Mothers and Daughters: Stories across a Generation, edited by Susan Koppelman. $9.95 paper.

Brown Girl, Brownstones, a novel by Paule Marshall. Afterword by Mary Helen Washington. $8.95 paper.

Call Home the Heart, a novel of the thirties, by Fielding Burke. Introduction by Alice Kessler-Harris and Paul Lauter and afterwords by Sylvia J. Cook and Anna W. Shannon. $9.95 paper.

Cassandra, by Florence Nightingale. Introduction by Myra Stark. Epilogue by Cynthia MacDonald. $4.50 paper.

The Changelings, a novel by Jo Sinclair. Afterwords by Nellie McKay, and Johnnetta B. Cole and Elizabeth H. Oakes; biographical note by Elisabeth Sandberg. $8.95 paper.

The Convert, a novel by Elizabeth Robins. Introduction by Jane Marcus. $8.95 paper.

Daddy Was a Number Runner, a novel by Louise Meriwether. Foreword by James Baldwin and afterword by Nellie McKay. $8.95 paper.

Daughter of the Hills: A Woman's Part in the Coal Miners' Struggle, a novel of the thirties, by Myra Page. Introduction by Alice Kessler-Harris and Paul Lauter and afterword by Deborah S. Rosenfelt. $8.95 paper.

An Estate of Memory, a novel by Ilona Karmel. Afterword by Ruth K. Angress. $11.95 paper.

Guardian Angel and Other Stories, by Margery Latimer. Afterwords by Nancy Loughridge, Meridel Le Sueur, and Louis Kampf. $8.95 paper.

I Love Myself when I Am Laughing . . . And Then Again when I Am Looking Mean and Impressive: A Zora Neale Hurston Reader, edited by Alice Walker. Introduction by Mary Helen Washington. $9.95 paper.

Life in the Iron Mills and Other Stories, by Rebecca Harding Davis. Biographical interpretation by Tillie Olsen. $7.95 paper.

The Living Is Easy, a novel by Dorothy West. Afterword by Adelaide M. Cromwell. $9.95 paper.

The Other Woman: Stories of Two Women and a Man. Edited by Susan Koppelman. $9.95 paper.

The Parish and the Hill, a novel by Mary Doyle Curran. Afterword by Anne Halley. $8.95 paper.

Reena and Other Stories, selected short stories by Paule Marshall. $8.95 paper.

Ripening: Selected Work, 1927-1980, 2nd edition, by Meridel Le Sueur. Edited with an introduction by Elaine Hedges. $9.95 paper.

Rope of Gold, a novel of the thirties, by Josephine Herbst. Introduction by Alice Kessler-Harris and Paul Lauter and afterword by Elinor Langer. $9.95 paper.

The Silent Partner, a novel by Elizabeth Stuart Phelps. Afterword by Mari Jo Buhle and Florence Howe. $8.95 paper.

Swastika Night, a novel by Katharine Burdekin. Introduction by Daphne Patai. $8.95 paper.

This Child's Gonna Live, a novel by Sarah E. Wright. Appreciation by John Oliver Killens. $9.95 paper.

The Unpossessed, a novel of the thirties, by Tess Slesinger. Introduction by Alice Kessler-Harris and Paul Lauter and afterword by Janet Sharistanian. $9.95 paper.

Weeds, a novel by Edith Summers Kelley. Afterword by Charlotte Goodman. $8.95 paper.

The Wide, Wide World, a novel by Susan Warner. Afterword by Jane Tompkins. $29.95 cloth, $11.95 paper.

A Woman of Genius, a novel by Mary Austin. Afterword by Nancy Porter. $9.95 paper.

Women and Appletrees, a novel by Moa Martinson. Translated from the Swedish and with an afterword by Margaret S. Lacy. $8.95 paper.

Women Working: An Anthology of Stories and Poems, edited and with an introduction by Nancy Hoffman and Florence Howe. $9.95 paper.

The Yellow Wallpaper, by Charlotte Perkins Gilman. Afterword by Elaine Hedges. $4.50 paper.

OTHER TITLES

Antoinette Brown Blackwell: A Biography, by Elizabeth Cazden. $24.95 cloth, $12.95 paper.

All the Women Are White, All the Blacks Are Men, but Some of Us Are Brave: Black Women's Studies, edited by Gloria T. Hull, Patricia Bell Scott, and Barbara Smith. $12.95 paper.

Black Foremothers: Three Lives, by Dorothy Sterling. $9.95 paper.

Complaints and Disorders: The Sexual Politics of Sickness, by Barbara Ehrenreich and Deirdre English. $3.95 paper.

The Cross-Cultural Study of Women, edited by Margot I. Duley and Mary I. Edwards. $29.95 cloth, $12.95 paper.

A Day at a Time: The Diary Literature of American Women from 1764 to the Present, edited and with an introduction by Margo Culley. $29.95 cloth, $12.95 paper.

The Defiant Muse: French Feminist Poems from the Middle Ages to the Present, a bilingual anthology edited and with an introduction by Domna C. Stanton. $29.95 cloth, $11.95 paper.

The Defiant Muse: German Feminist Poems from the Middle Ages to the Present, a bilingual anthology edited and with an introduction by Susan L. Cocalis. $29.95 cloth, $11.95 paper.

The Defiant Muse: Hispanic Feminist Poems from the Middle Ages to the Present, a bilingual anthology edited and with an introduction by Angel Flores and Kate Flores. $29.95 cloth, $11.95 paper.

The Defiant Muse: Italian Feminist Poems from the Middle Ages to the Present, a bilingual anthology edited by Beverly Allen, Muriel Kittel, and Keala Jane Jewell, and with an introduction by Beverly Allen. $29.95 cloth, $11.95 paper.

Feminist Resources for Schools and Colleges: A Guide to Curricular Materials, 3rd edition, compiled and edited by Anne Chapman. $12.95 paper.

Household and Kin, 2nd ed. (formerly *Families in Flux*), by Amy Swerdlow, Renate Bridenthal, Joan Kelly, and Phyllis Vine. $9.95 paper.

How to Get Money for Research, by Mary Rubin and the Business and Professional Women's Foundation. Foreword by Mariam Chamberlain. $6.95 paper.

In Her Own Image: Women Working in the Arts, edited and with an introduction by Elaine Hedges and Ingrid Wendt. $9.95 paper.

Integrating Women's Studies into the Curriculum: A Guide and Bibliography, by Betty Schmitz. $9.95 paper.

Käthe Kollwitz: Woman and Artist, by Martha Kearns, $9.95 paper.

Las Mujeres: Conversations from a Hispanic Community, by Nan Elsasser, Kyle MacKenzie, and Yvonne Tixier y Vigil. $9.95 paper.

Lesbian Studies: Present and Future, edited by Margaret Cruikshank. $9.95 paper.

Mother to Daughter, Daughter to Mother: A Daybook and Reader, selected and shaped by Tillie Olsen. $9.95 paper.

Moving the Mountain: Women Working for Social Change, by Ellen Cantarow with Susan Gushee O'Malley and Sharon Hartman Strom. $9.95 paper.

Out of the Bleachers: Writings on Women and Sport, edited and with an introduction by Stephanie L. Twin. $10.95 paper.

Portraits of Chinese Women in Revolution, by Agnes Smedley. Edited and with an introduction by Jan MacKinnon and Steve MacKinnon and an afterword by Florence Howe. $10.95 paper.

Reconstructing American Literature: Courses, Syllabi, Issues, edited by Paul Lauter. $10.95 paper.

Rights and Wrongs: Women's Struggle for Legal Equality, 2nd edition, by Susan Cary Nichols, Alice M. Price, and Rachel Rubin. $7.95 paper.

Salt of the Earth, screenplay by Michael Wilson with historical commentary by Deborah Silverton Rosenfelt. $10.95 paper.

These Modern Women: Autobiographical Essays from the Twenties, edited with an introduction by Elaine Showalter. $8.95 paper.

Witches, Midwives, and Nurses: A History of Women Healers, by Barbara Ehrenreich and Deirdre English. $3.95 paper.

With These Hands: Women Working on the Land, edited with an introduction by Joan M. Jensen. $9.95 paper.

The Woman and the Myth: Margaret Fuller's Life and Writings, by Bell Gale Chevigny. $8.95 paper.

Woman's "True" Profession: Voices from the History of Teaching, edited with an introduction by Nancy Hoffman. $9.95 paper.

Women Have Always Worked: A Historical Overview, by Alice Kessler-Harris. $9.95 paper.

For a free catalog, write to The Feminist Press at The City University of New York, 311 East 94 Street, New York, NY 10128. Send individual book orders to The Talman Company, Inc., 150 Fifth Avenue, New York, NY 10011. Please include $1.75 for postage and handling for one book, $.75 for each additional.